It's a Jungle Out There

humor and wisdom for living and loving life

PuddleDancer PRESS™

Created by Meiji Stewart

Illustrated by David Blaisdell

It's a Jungle Out There!
© 1996 by Meiji Stewart

ISBN# 0-9647349-5-8

PuddleDancer Press is an imprint of the
Keep Coming Back Company.
Published in Del Mar, California
P.O. Box 1204, Del Mar, California 92014
619-452-1386

1st Printing

Illustration: David Blaisdell, Tucson, Arizona
Cover design: Kahn Design, Encinitas, California
Book design: Endore, Ink., San Diego, California
Printing: Vaughan Printing, Nashville, Tennessee

Dedicated to:
My mother, Nannette, and father, Richard, my sister, Leslie, my brothers, Ray and Scott, my nephews and nieces Sebastien, Emilie, Skye, Luke, Jake, Nannette, Cairo and Kamana, and to Fumi, Jocelyne, Richard and Stephen. And especially to my daughter Malia (the puddledancer), and her loving mom, Julie.

Thanks to:
David for the wonderful illustrations. I am blessed to be able to work with him. Thanks also to Roger and Gita for putting it all together, almost always under deadline (usually yesterday). Thanks to Jeff for the delightful book covers, and, even more, for his friendship. Thanks to Julie, Gay, Jane, Regina, Rich and Zane for making it possible to bring PuddleDancer Press to life. And thanks to my mom and dad for encouraging me to pursue my dreams.

You have brains in your head.
You have feet in your shoes.
You can steer yourself
Any direction you choose.

Dr. Seuss

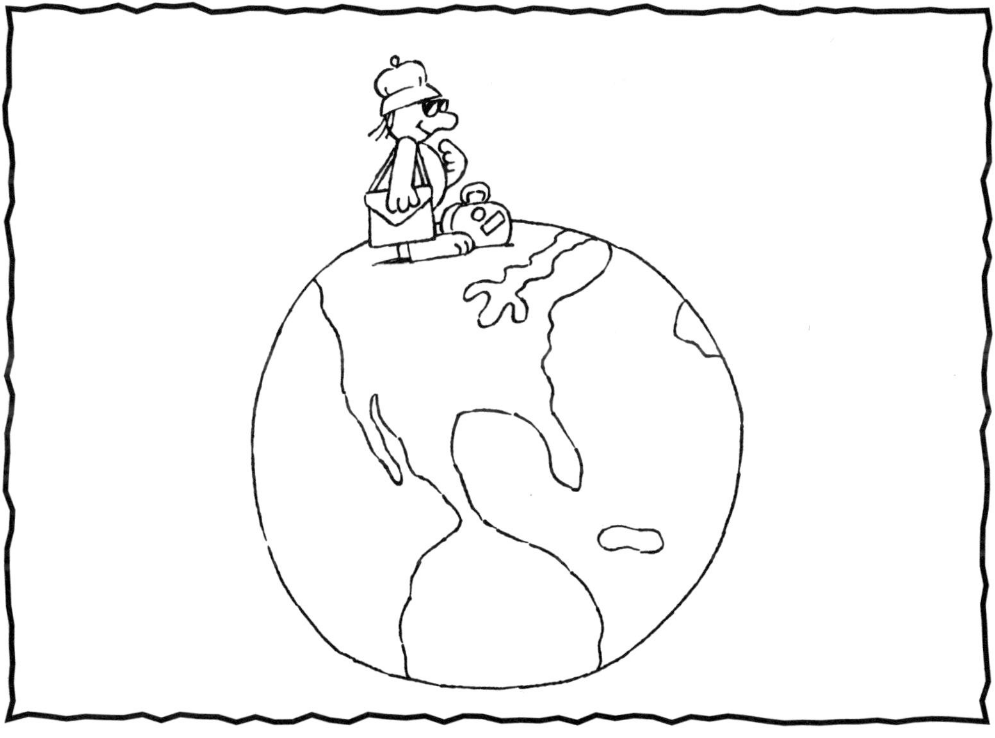

Friends are the most wonderful gifts
we can give ourselves.

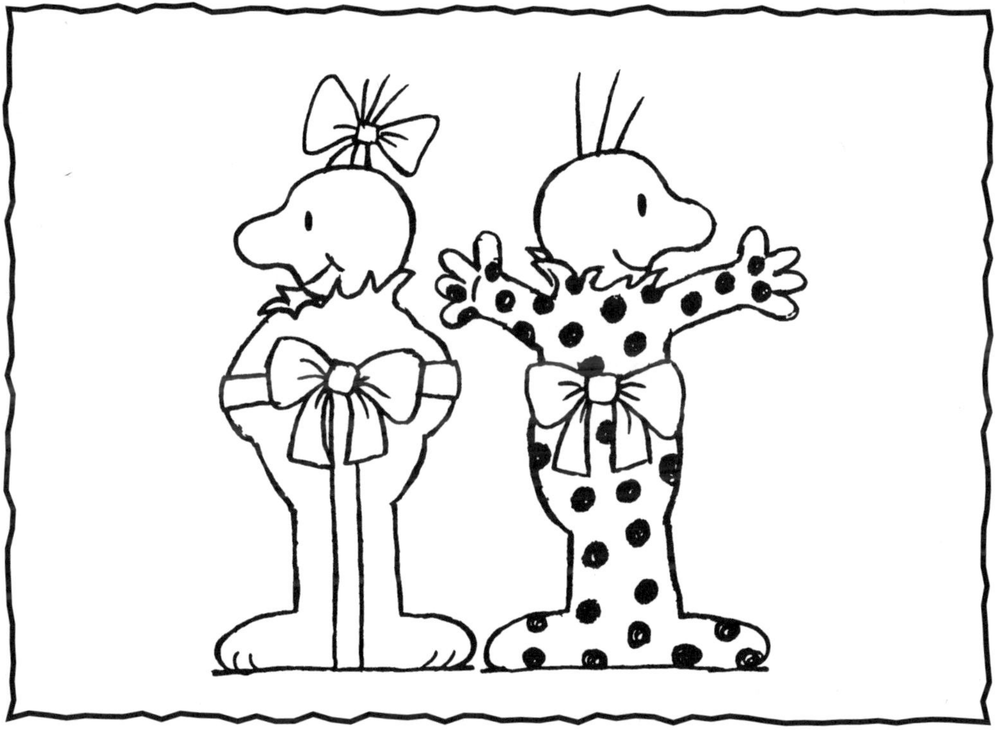

Most people are as happy as they
make up their minds to be.

Abraham Lincoln

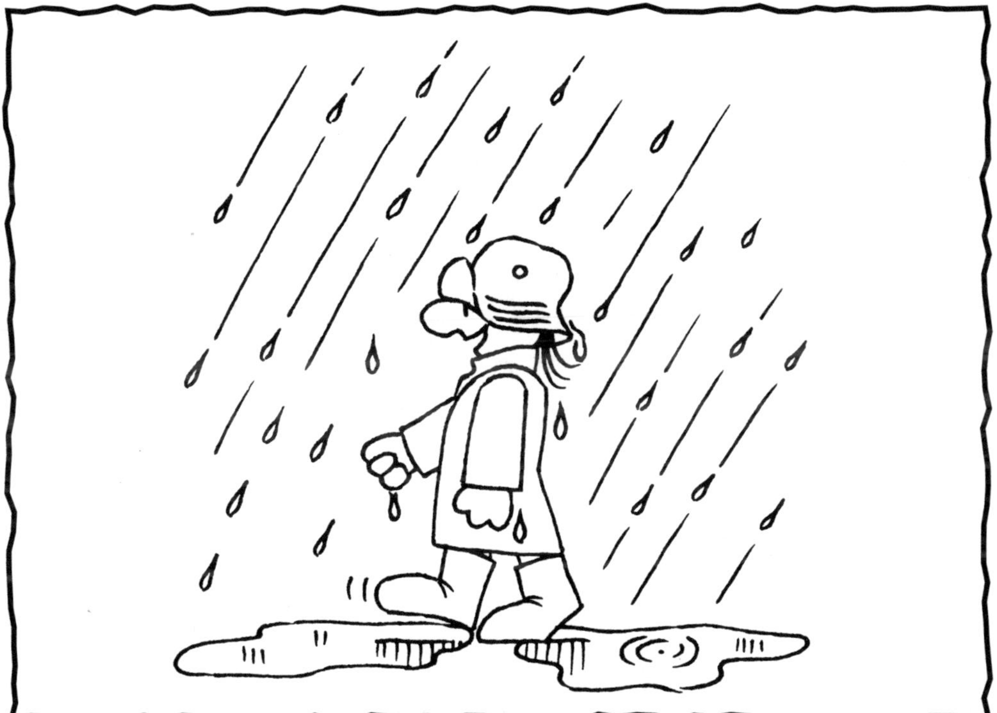

For every ailment under the sun,
There is a remedy, or there is none:
If there be one, try to find it;
If there is none, never mind it.

A great life is the sum total of the
worthwhile things you've been
doing one by one. Those who pluck
a flower here and there
soon have a bouquet.

Richard Bach

Express yourself.

10

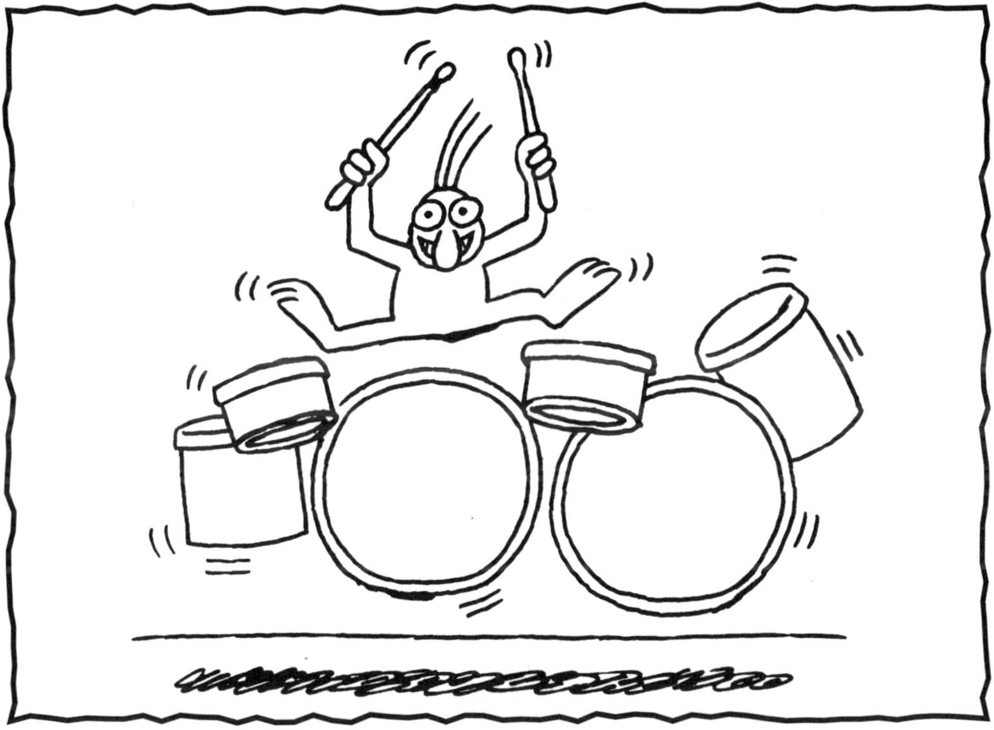

Why hoard your troubles?
They have no market value,
so just throw them away.

Ann Schade

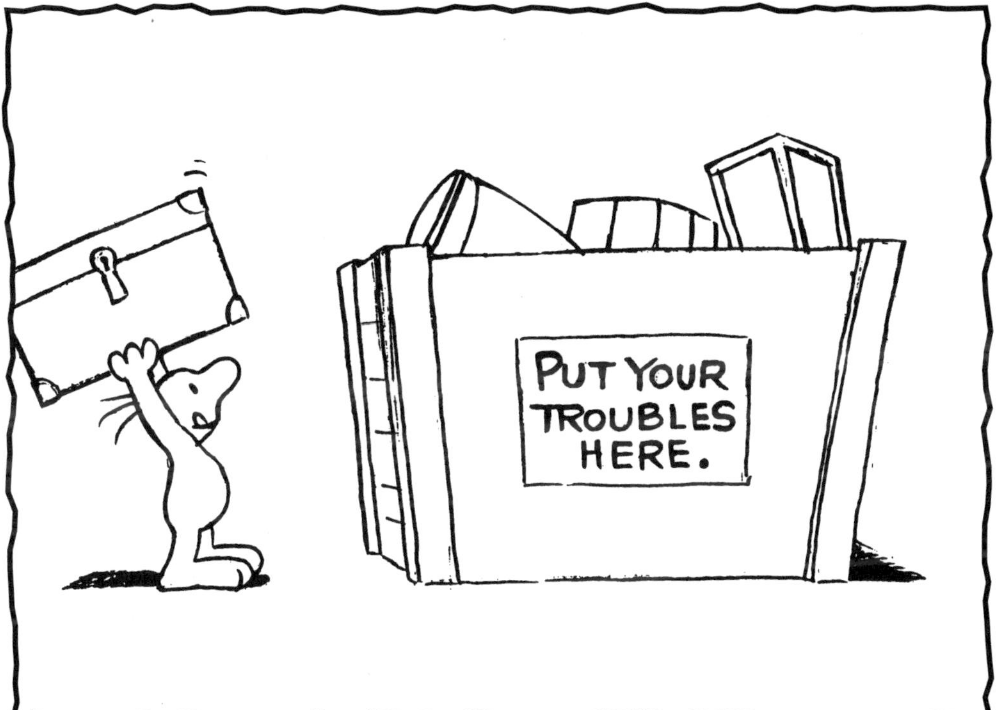
PUT YOUR TROUBLES HERE.

If you would be loved,
love and be loveable

Benjamin Franklin

It is never too late to be
what you might have been.

George Eliot

Either you let your life slip away by
not doing the things you want to
do, or you get up and do them.

Carl Ally

16

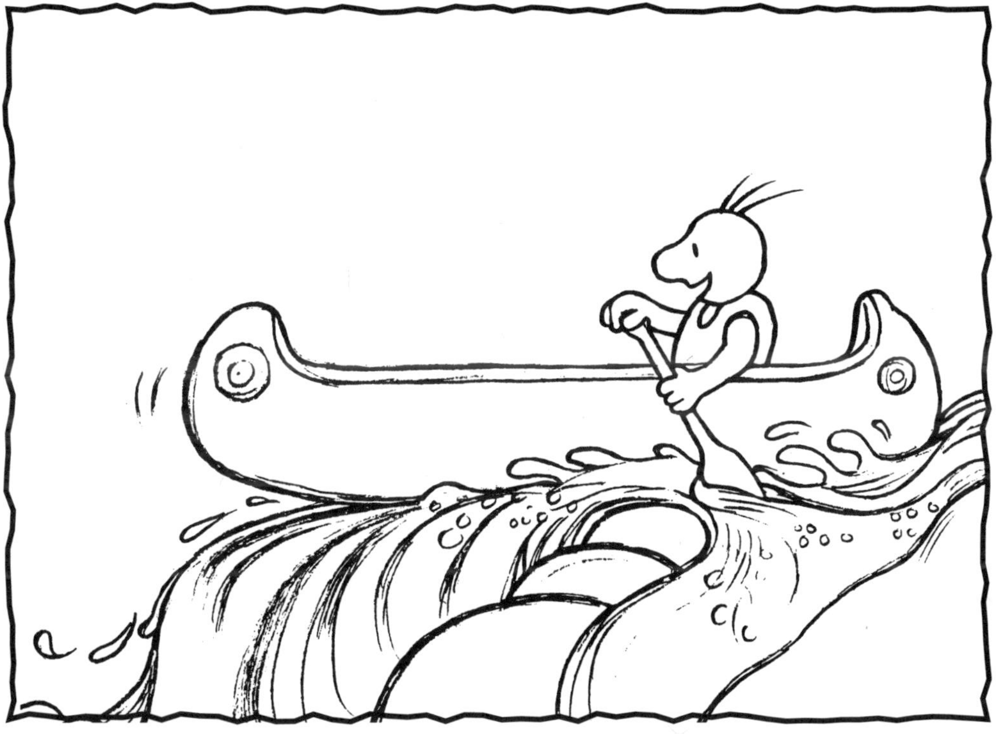

Reflect upon your present blessings,
of which every man has many –
not on your past misfortunes, of
which all men have some.

Charles Dickens

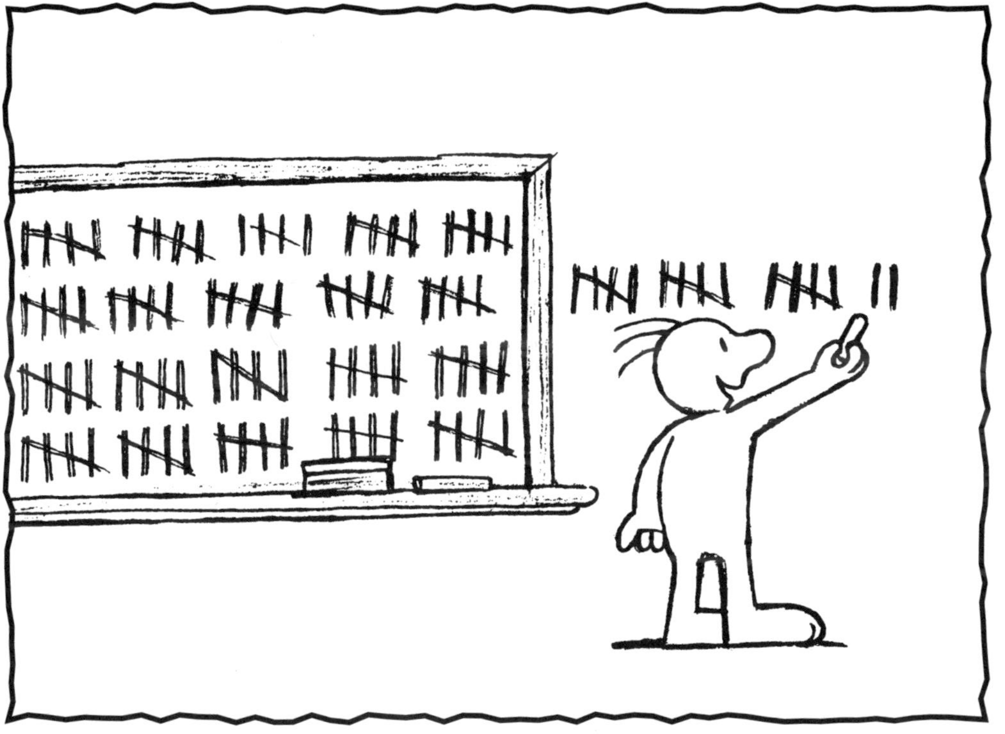

If we could read the secret history of our
enemies we would find in each man's
life a sorrow and a suffering
enough to disarm all hostility.

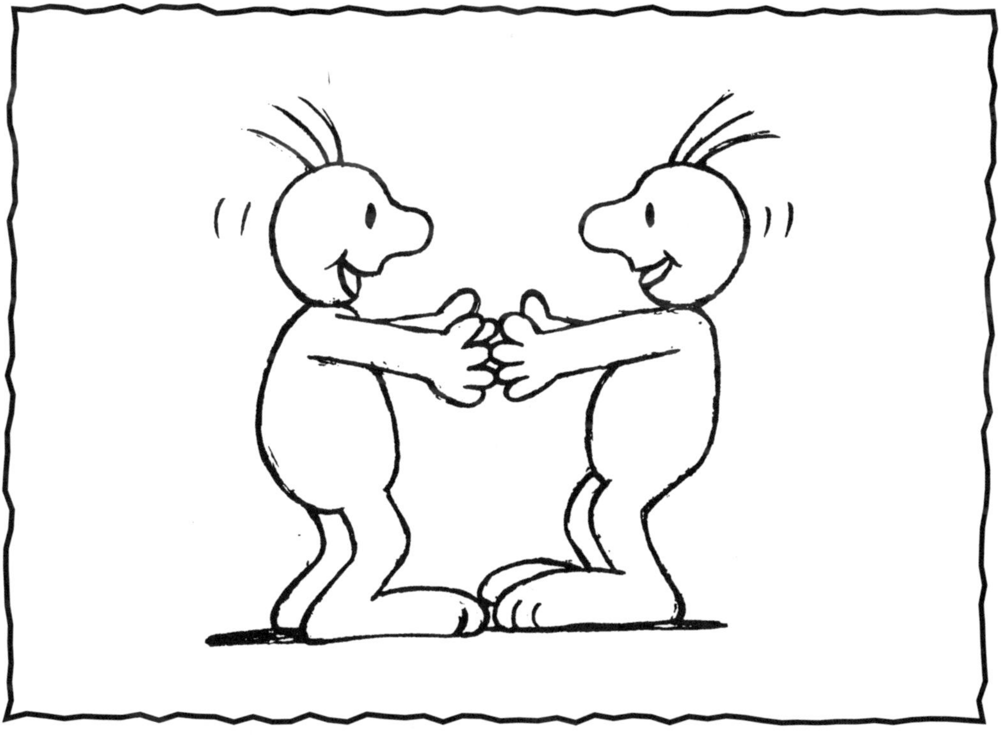

The chief danger in life is that you
may take too many precautions.

Alfred Adler

It takes courage to lead a life.
Any life.

Erica Jong

23

The important thing is not to stop
questioning. Curiosity has its own
reasoning for existing... Never lose a
holy curiosity.

Albert Einstein

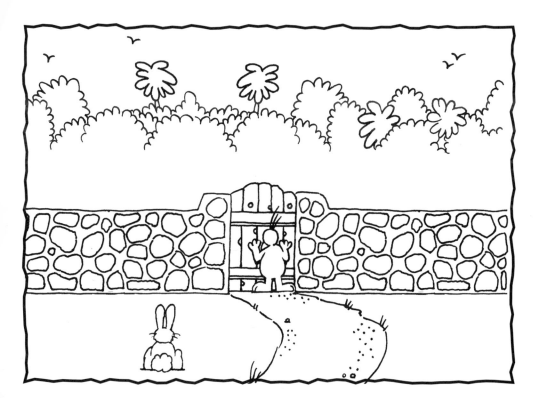

If God is your co-pilot – move over.

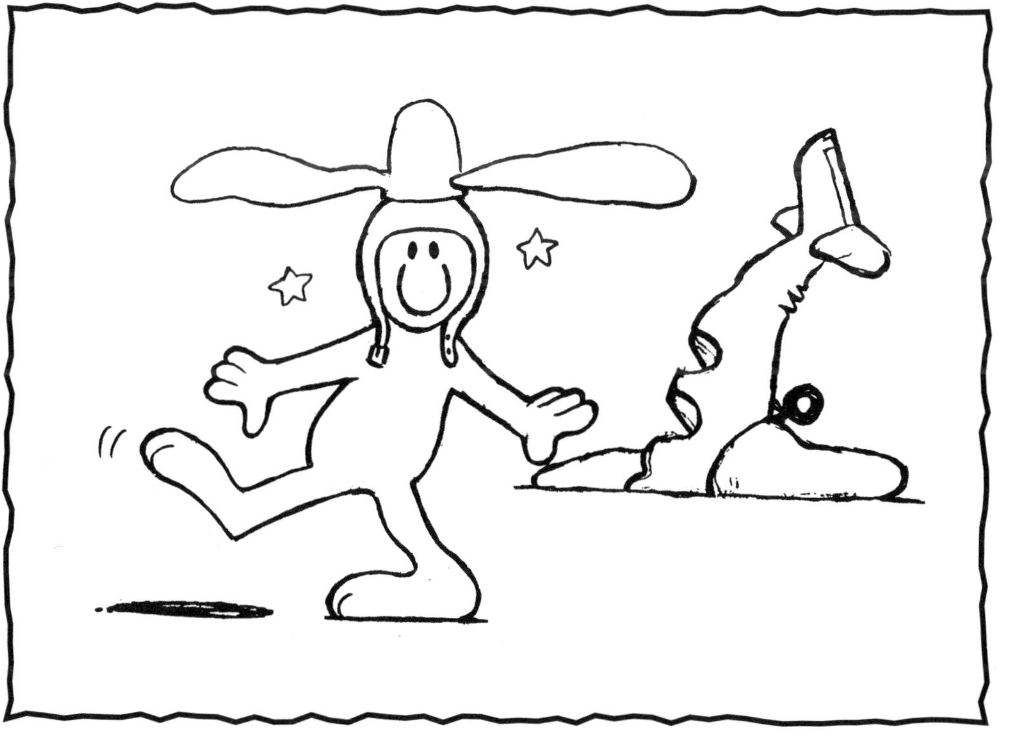

We must care about the world
of our children and grandchildren,
a world we may never see.

Bertrand Russell

In all my years of counseling those near death, I've yet to hear anyone say they wish they had spent more time at the office.

Rabbi Kuschner

The way I see it, if you want the rainbow,
you gotta put up with the rain.

Dolly Parton

30

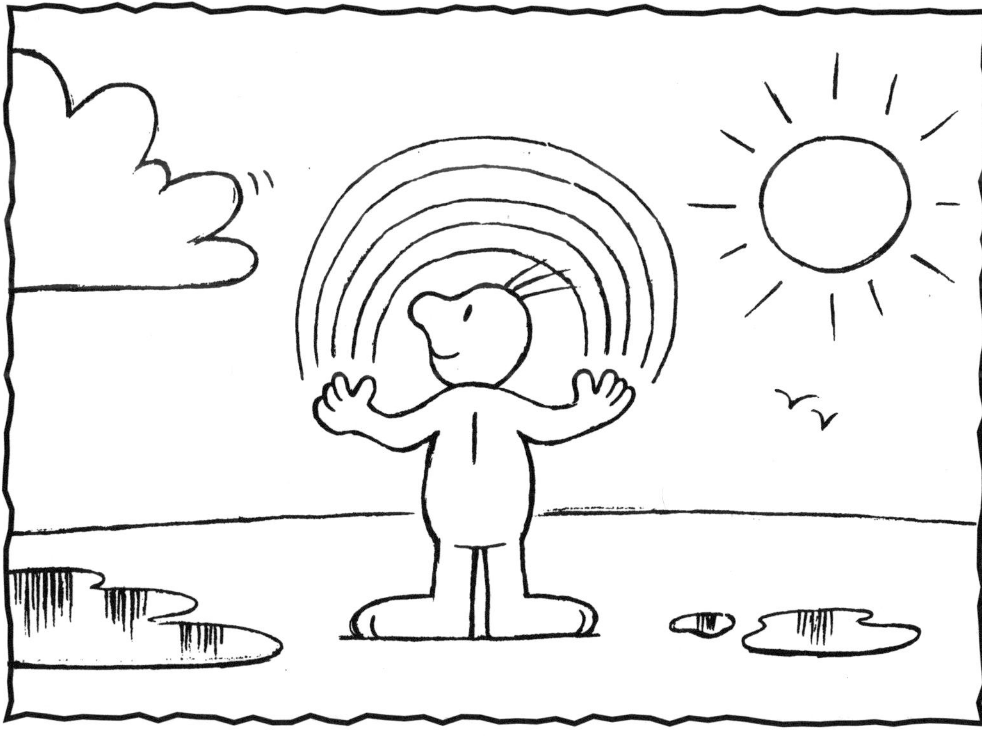

I have enough money to last me the rest
of my life, unless I buy something.

Jackie Mason

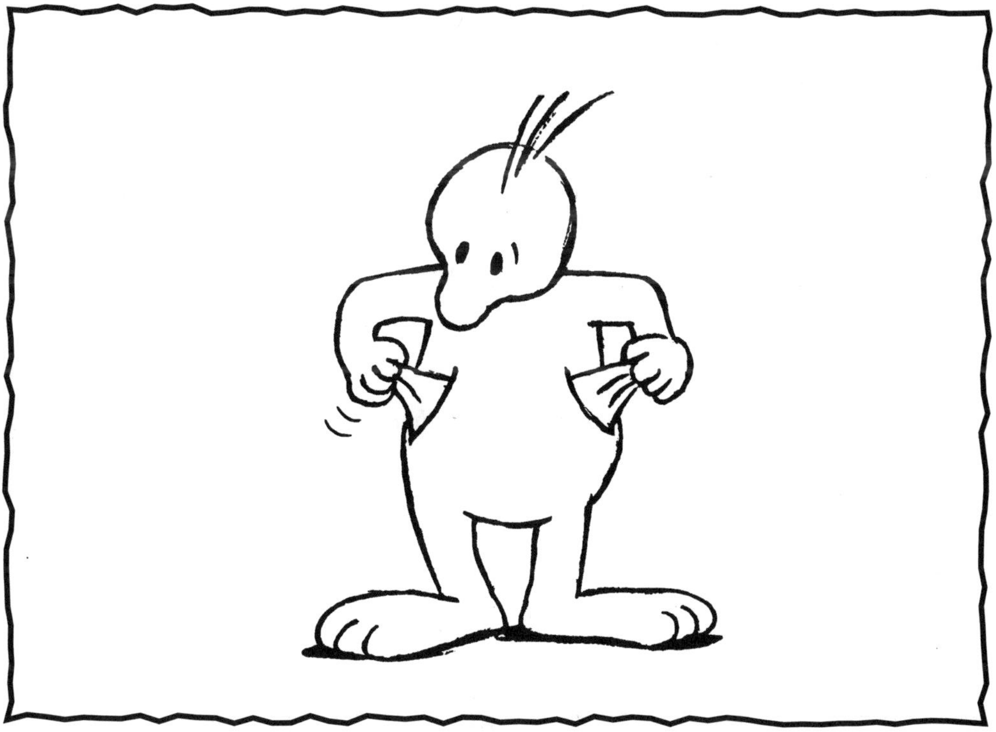

Rest is not a matter of doing
absolutely nothing. Rest is repair.

Daniel W. Josselyn

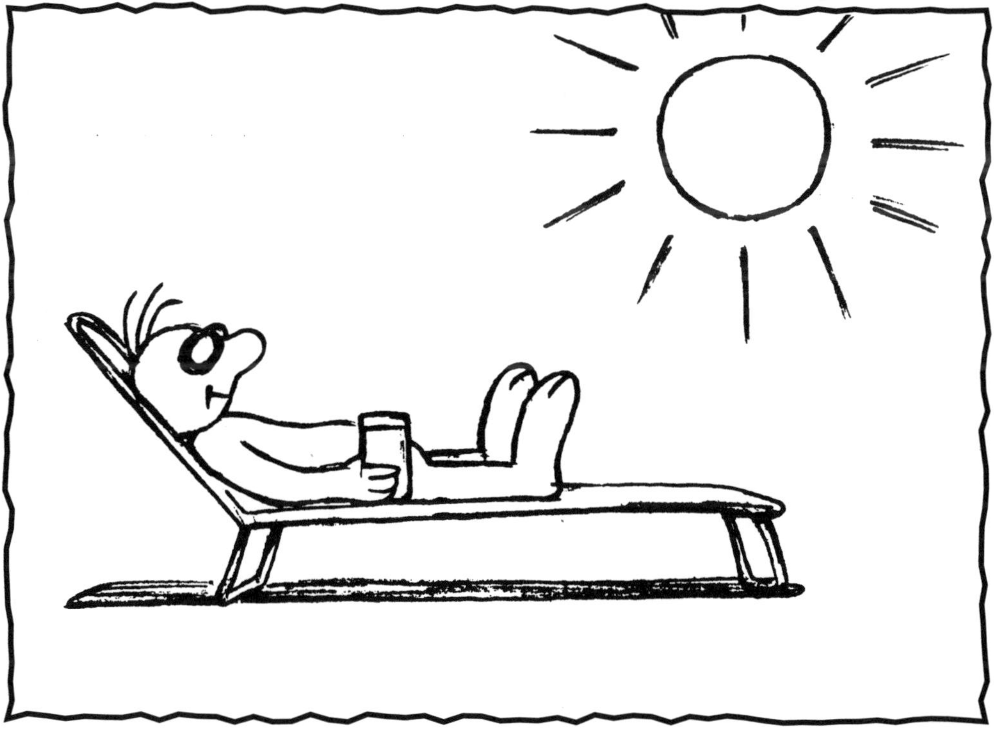

Love doesn't make the world go 'round.
Love is what makes the ride worthwhile.

Audrey Woodhall

The trouble with life is, you're
halfway through it before you
realize it's a 'do it yourself' thing.

Annie Zadra

Be glad of life because it gives you
the chance to love and to work and
to play and to look up at the stars.

Henry Van Dyke

38

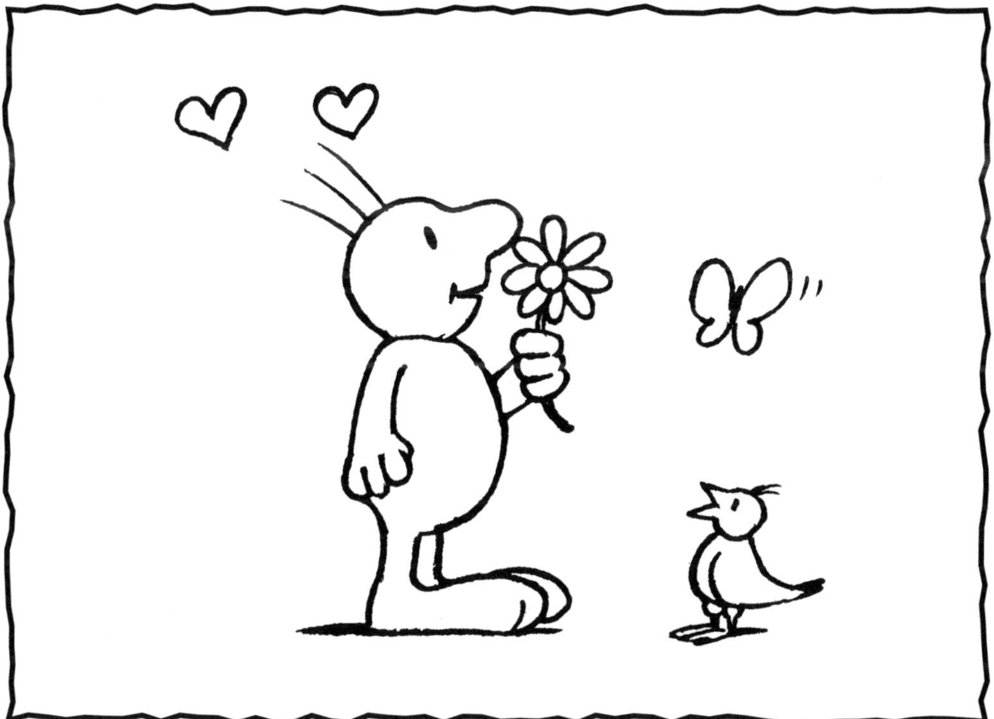

If you can't be thankful for
what you receive, be thankful for
what you escape.

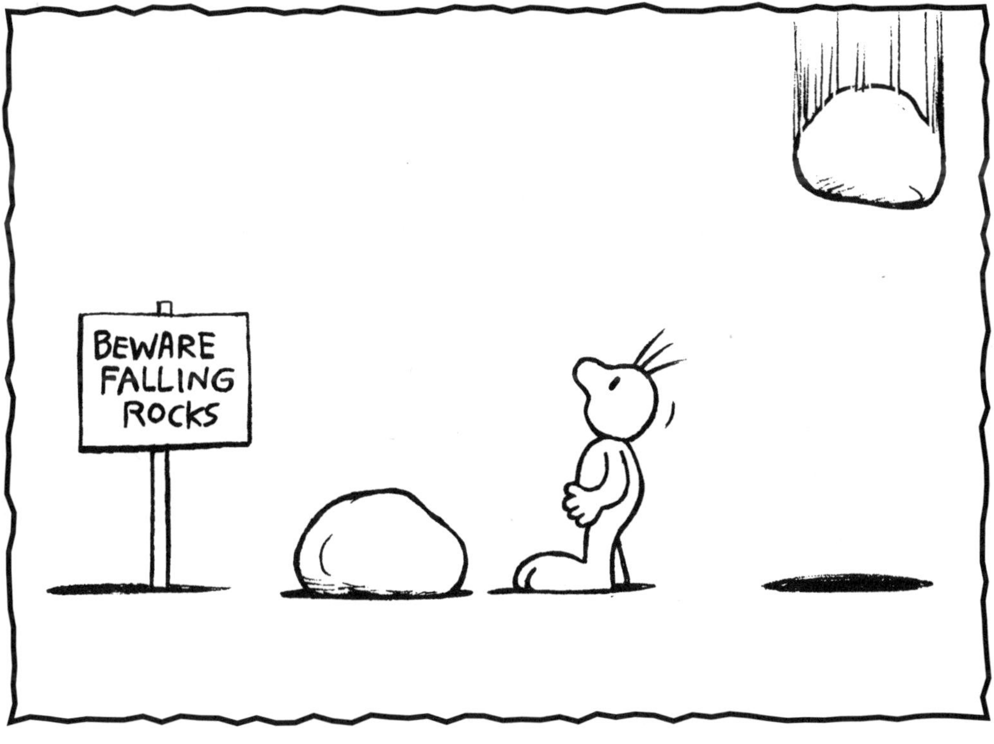
BEWARE
FALLING
ROCKS

A tulip doesn't strive to impress anyone.
It doesn't struggle to be different than a rose.
It doesn't have to. It is different.
And there is room in the garden for every flower.

Marianne Williamson

Everyday courage has few witnesses.
But yours is not less noble because
no drum beats before you, and no
crowds shout your name.

Robert Louis Stevenson

43

You cannot shake hands
with a clenched fist.

Indira Gandhi

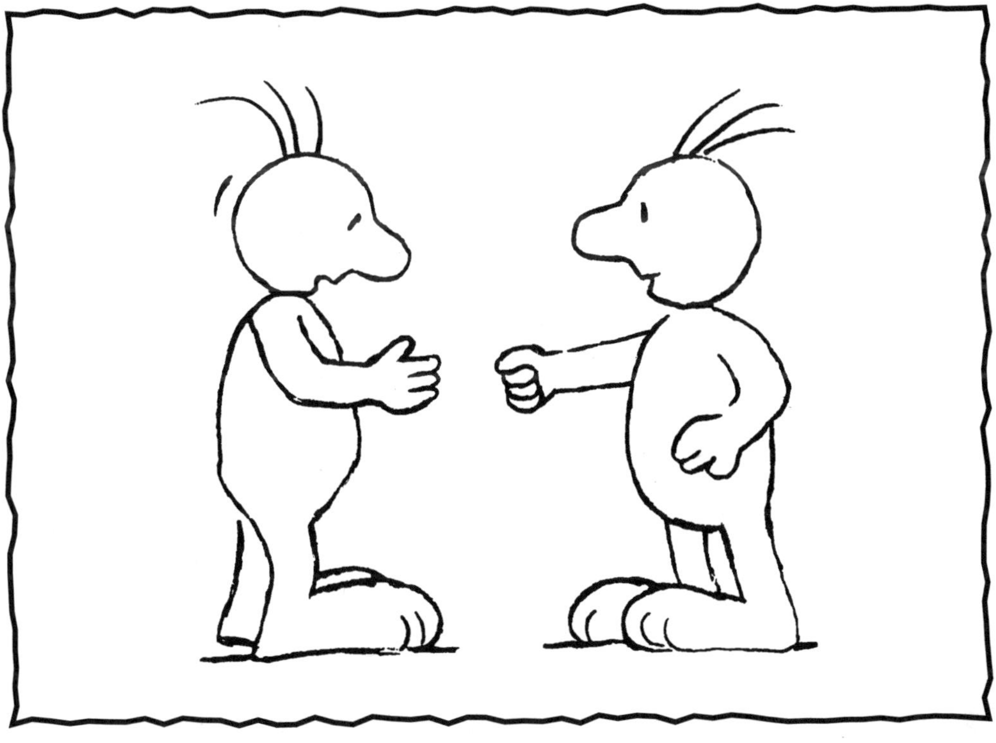

It is one of the most beautiful
compensations of this life that no
man can sincerely try to help
another without helping himself.

Ralph Waldo Emerson

46

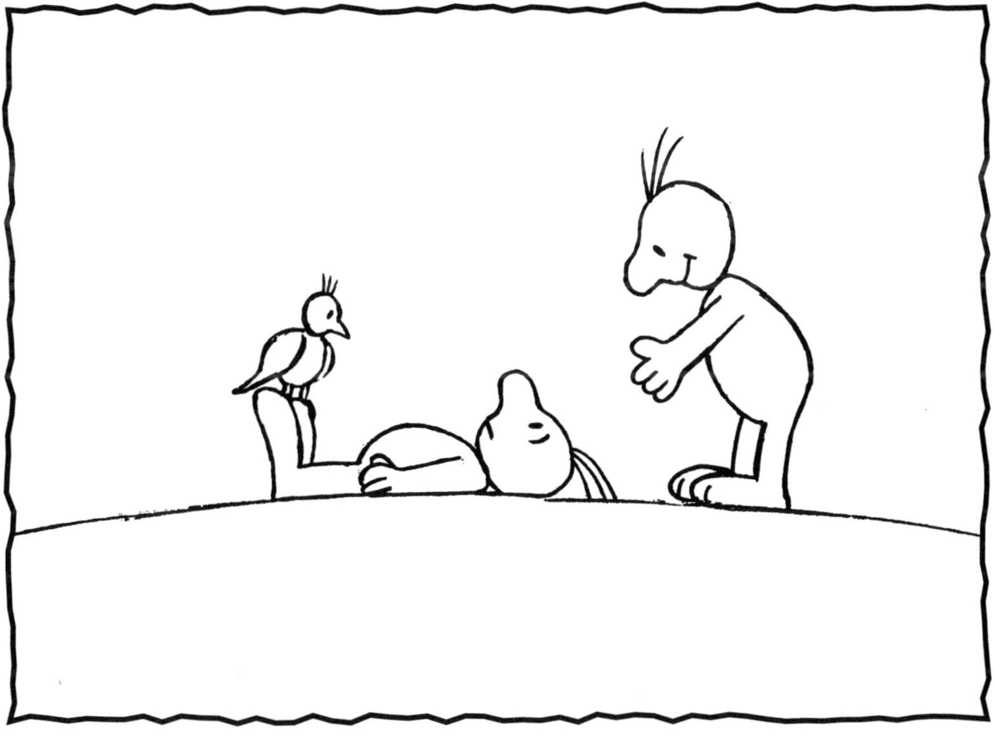

Our greatest glory is not in never falling,
But in rising every time we fall.

Confucius

48

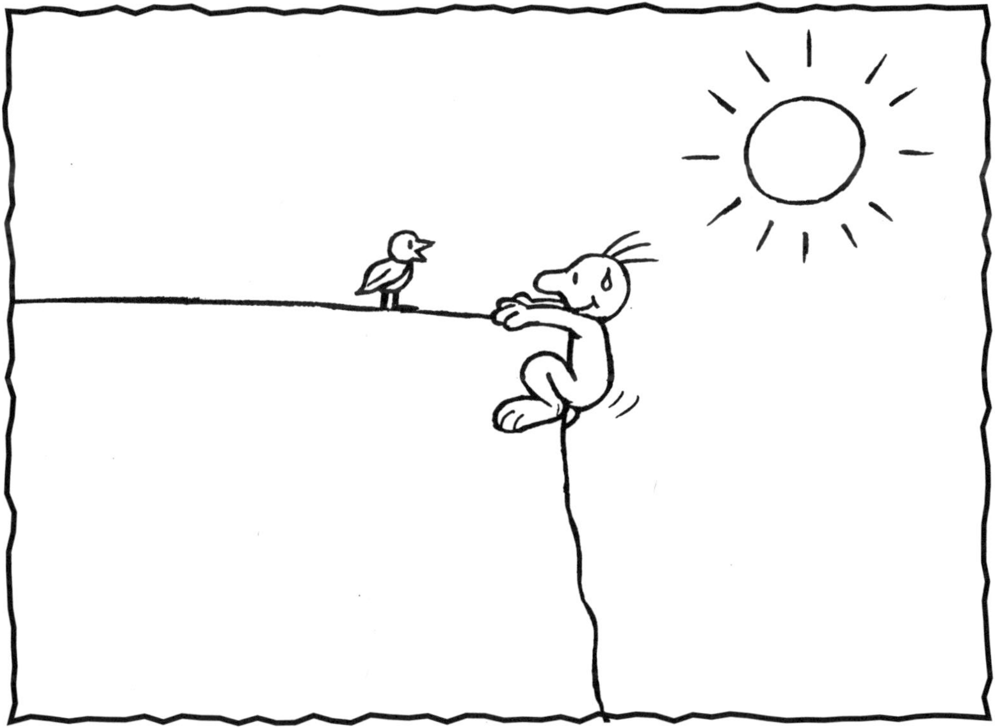

The journey in between what you once were and who you are now becoming is where the dance of life really takes place.

Barbara De Angelis

Of all the people you will know in a lifetime,
you are the only one you will never leave nor lose.
To the question of your life, you are the only answer.
To the problems of your life, you are the only solution.

Jo Coudert

A man has made at least a start on
discovering the meaning of life when he
plants shade trees under which he
knows full well he will never sit.

Elton Trueblood

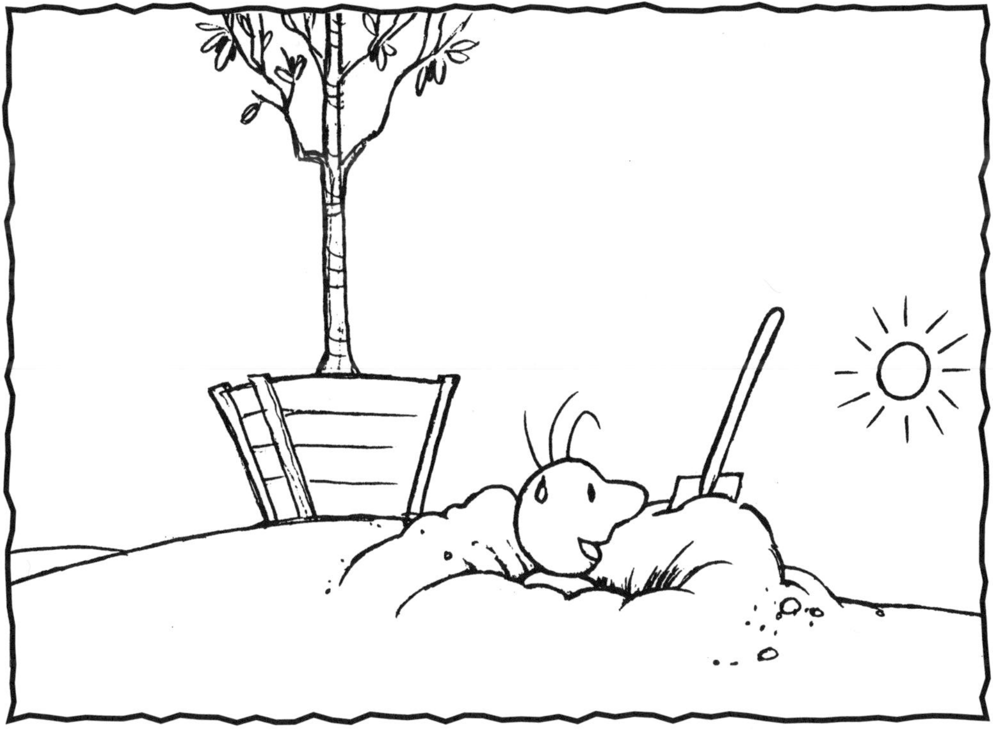

If you judge people, you have
no time to love them.

Mother Teresa

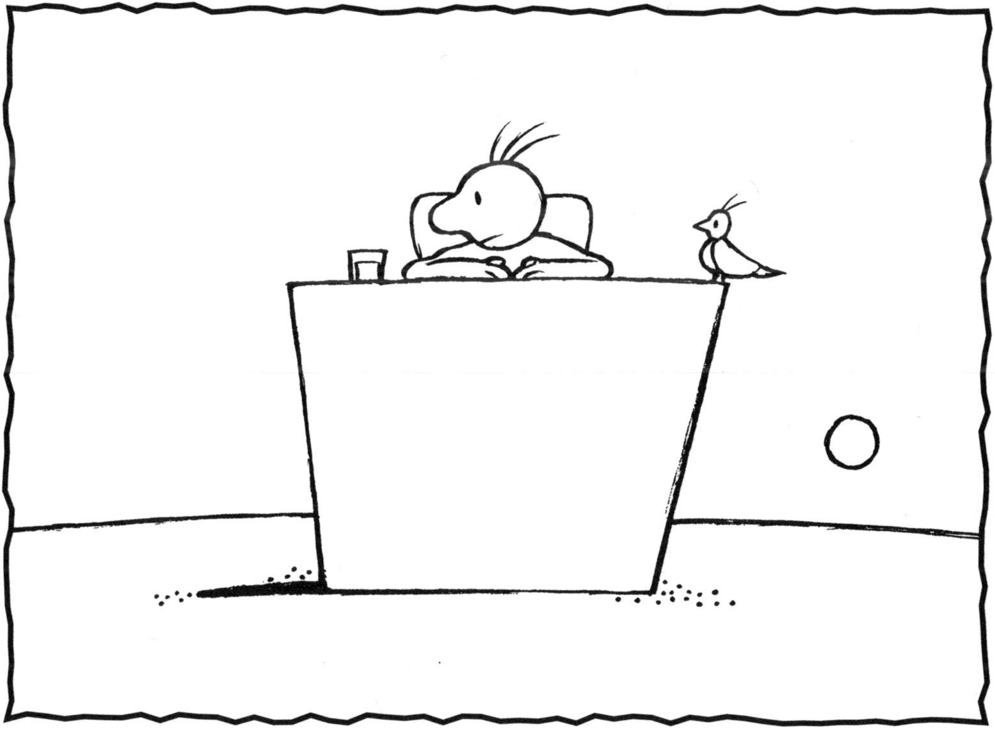

A man should never be ashamed to
say he has been wrong, which is
but saying in other words that he is
wiser today than he was yesterday.

Alexander Pope

When you grow old or ill, the most
important things to you will be who
and what you've loved.

June Martin

This too shall pass

King Solomon

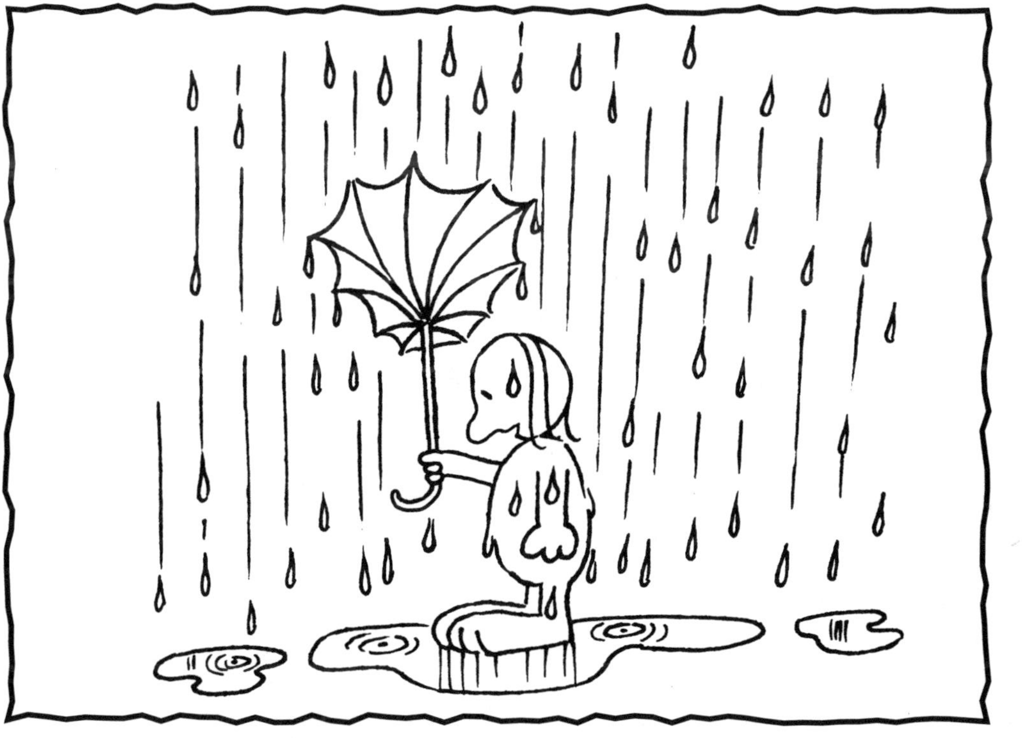

There are many wonderful things
that will never be done if you do
not do them.

Charles D. Gill

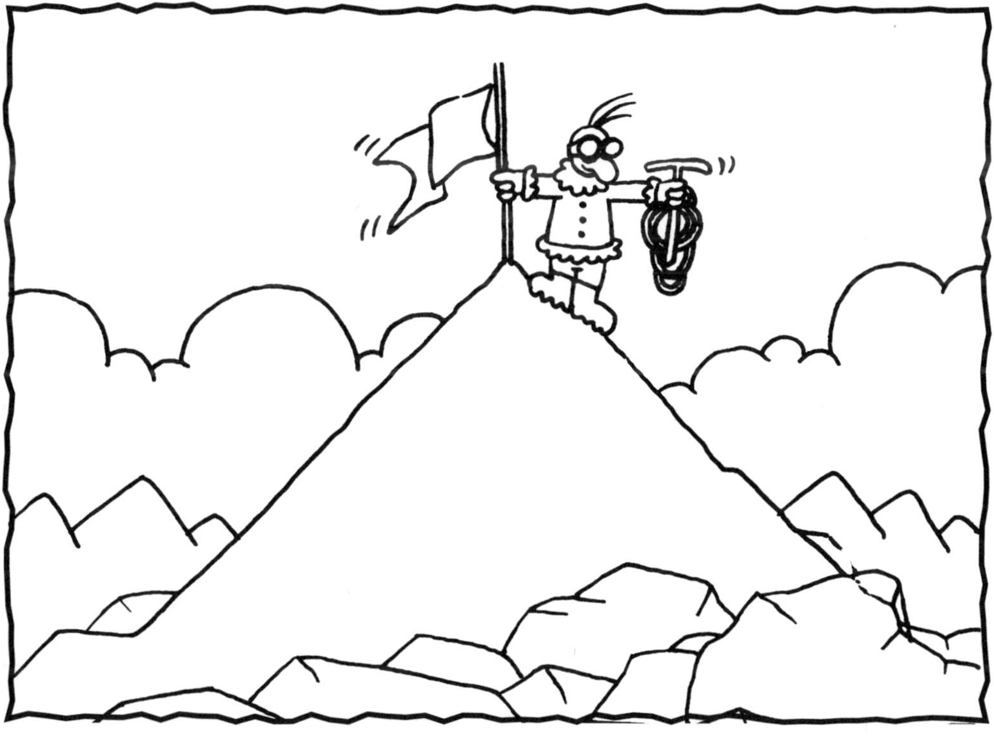

Kind words can be short and easy to speak,
but their echoes are endless.

Mother Teresa

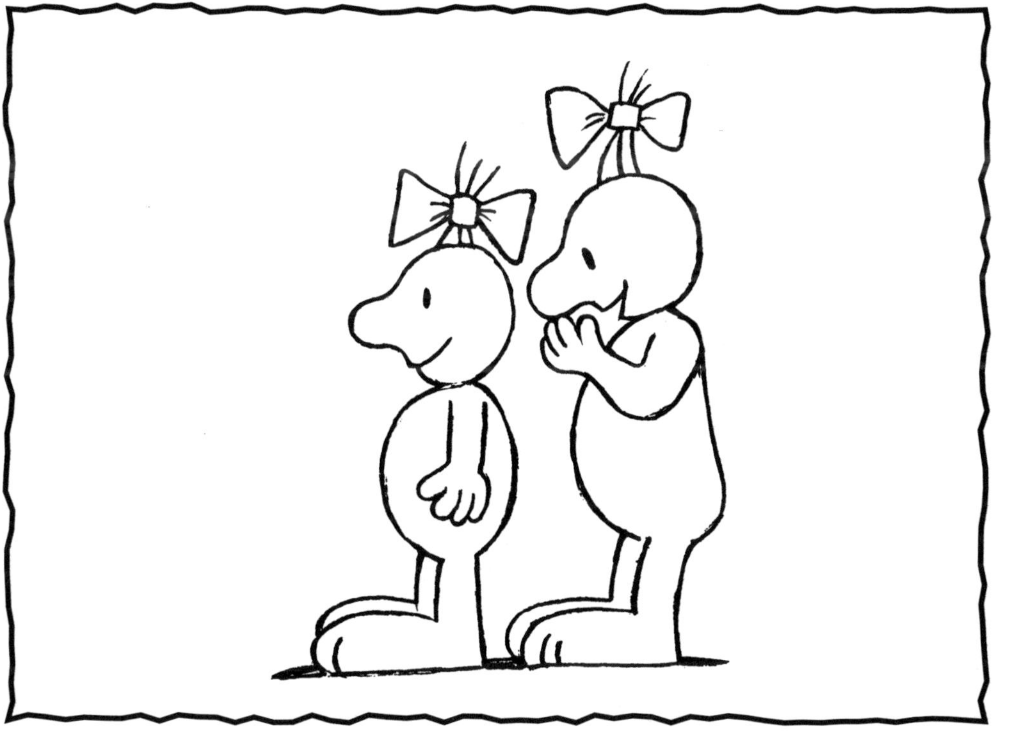

I am only one, but still I am one.
I cannot do everything,
but still I can do something.
And because I cannot do everything,
I will not refuse to do the something I can do.

Helen Keller

It is one thing to show a man that
he is in error, and another to put
him in possession of truth.

John Locke

Angels can fly because they
take themselves lightly.

G.K. Chesterton

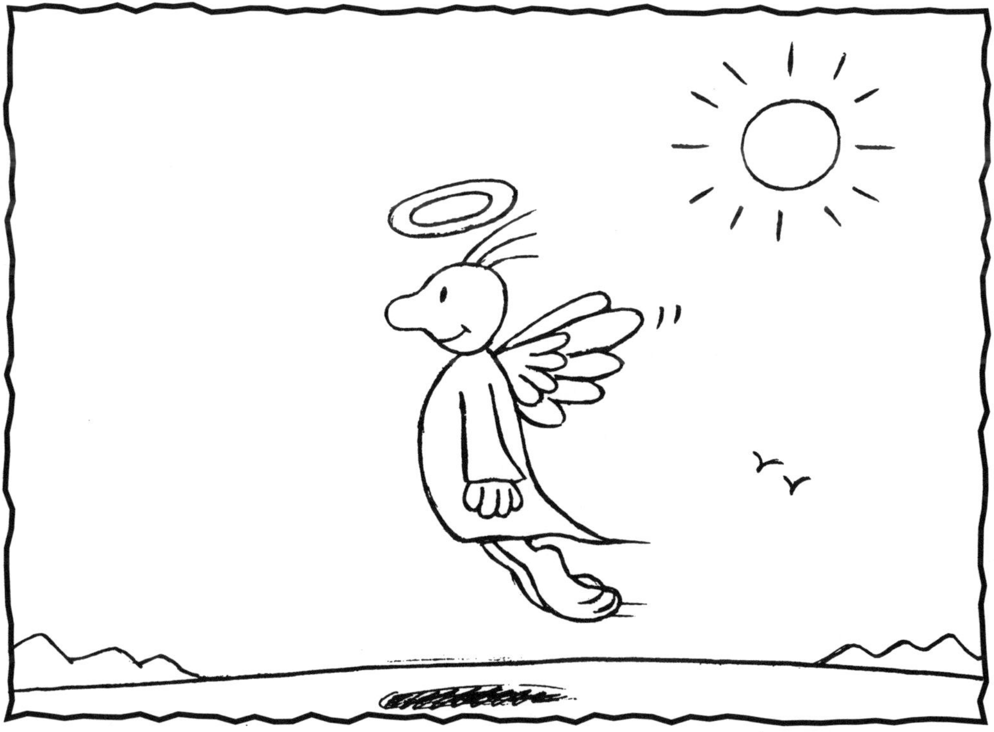

I find the great thing in this world
is not so much where we stand, as
in what direction we are moving:
To reach the port of Heaven we
must sail, sometimes with the wind
and sometime against it- but we
must sail, not drift or lie at anchor.

Oliver Wendell Holmes, Jr

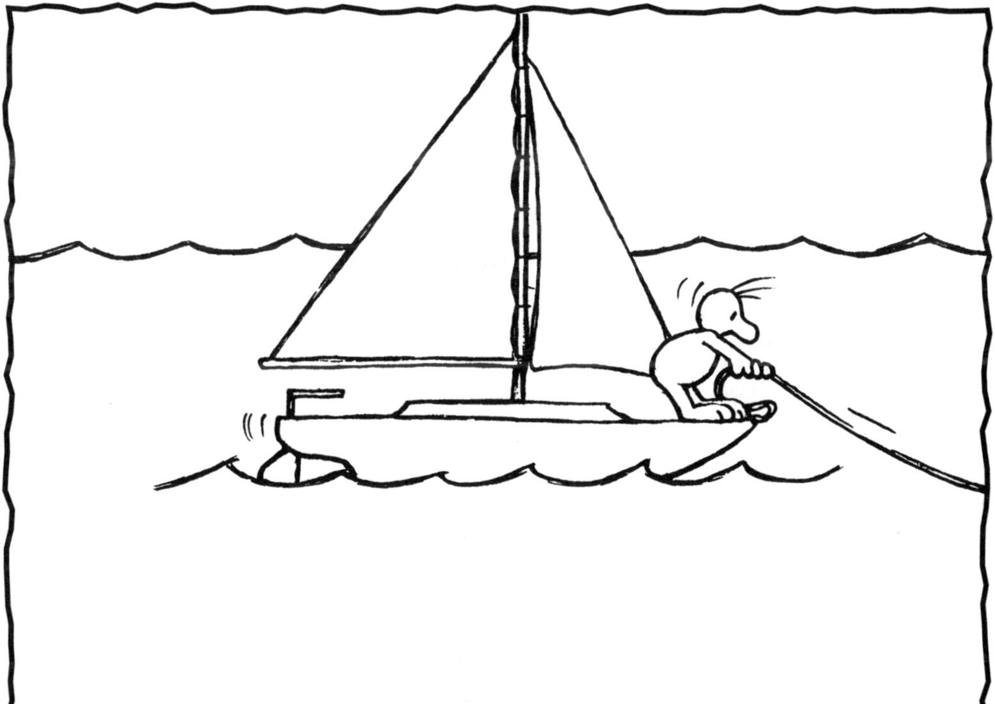

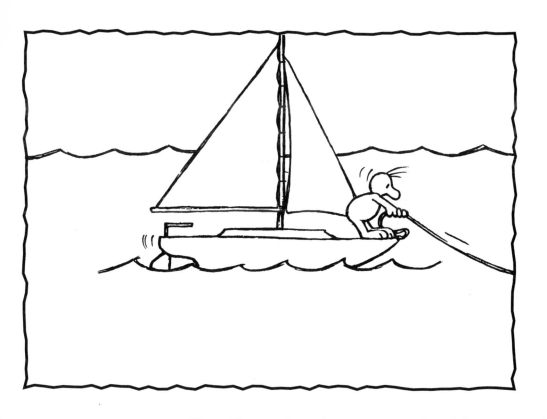

Many people think that if they were
only in some other place, or had some
other job, they would be happy. Well,
that is doubtful. So get as much
happiness out of what you are doing
as you can and don't put off being
happy until some future date.

Dale Carnegie

Nobody ever has it "all together."
That's like trying to eat
"once and for all."

Marilyn Grey

Exactly what part of the word "no"
don't you understand?

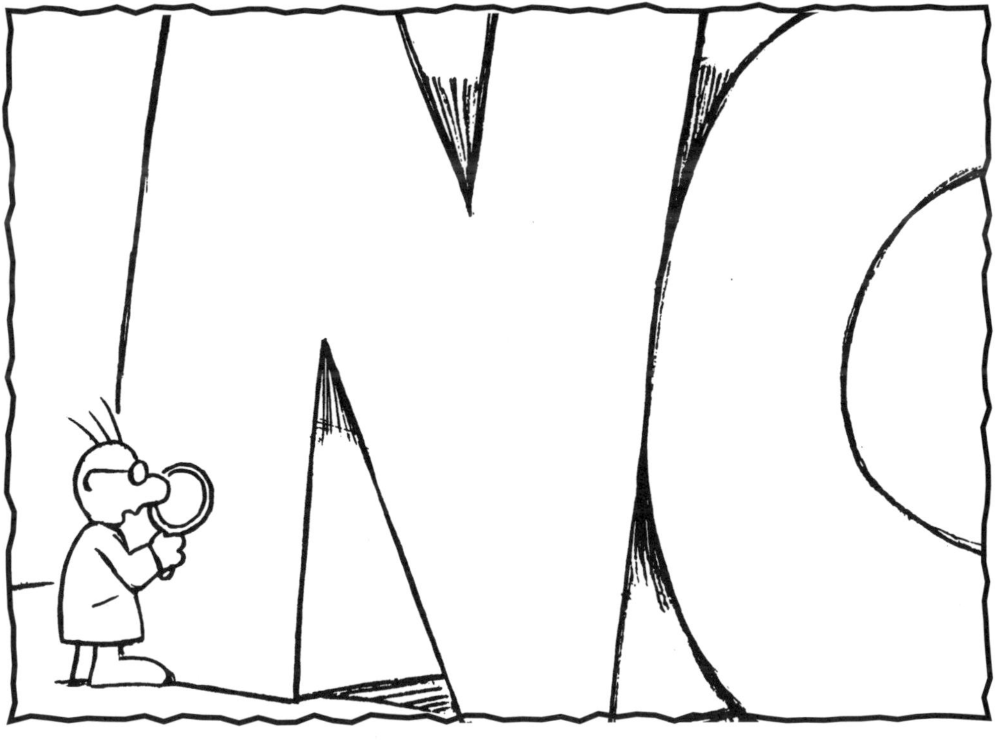

It's a jungle out there!

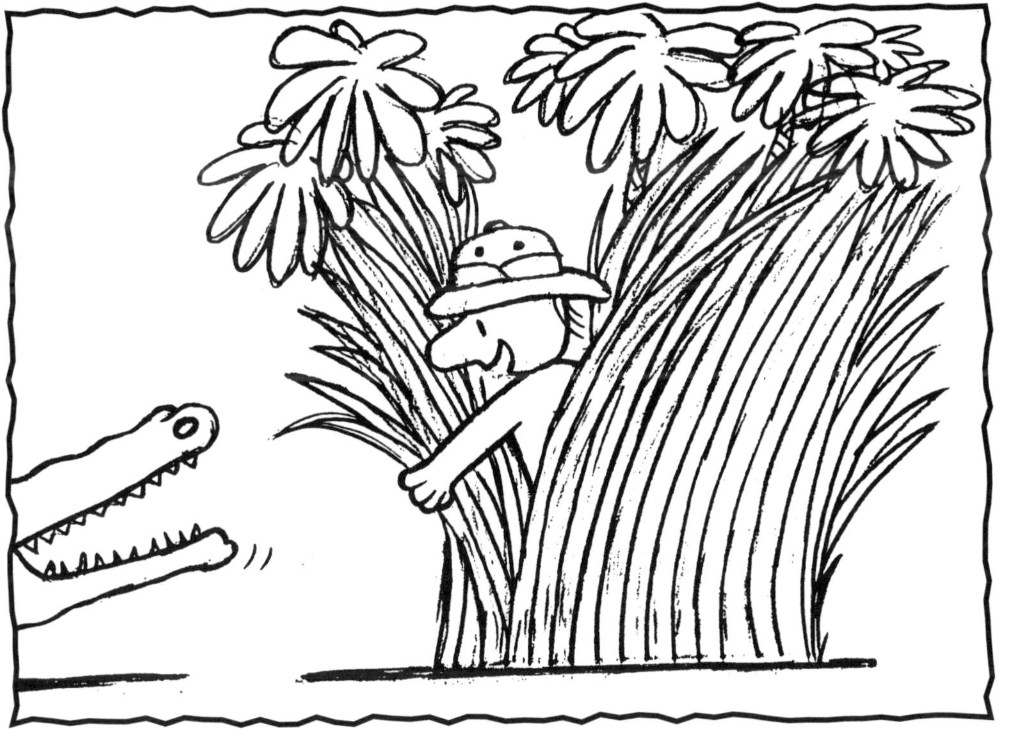

Warning! Carrying a grudge can be
harmful to your health.

G.M. Stewart

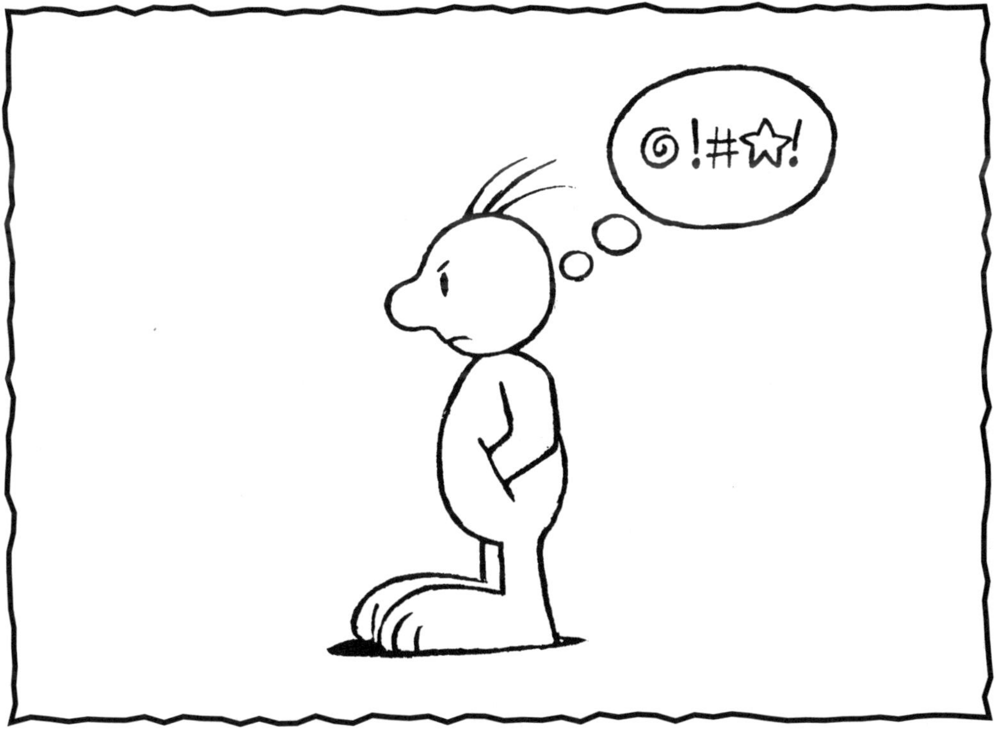

If Spring came but once in a century
instead of once a year, or burst
forth with the sound of an
earthquake and not in silence, what
wonder and expectation there would
be in all hearts, to behold the
miraculous change.

Henry Wadsworth Longfellow

There are four ways
God answers prayer:
No, not yet;
No, I love you too much;
Yes, I thought you'd never ask;
Yes, and here's more.

Ann Lewis

A true friend is a fowl
weather friend.

80

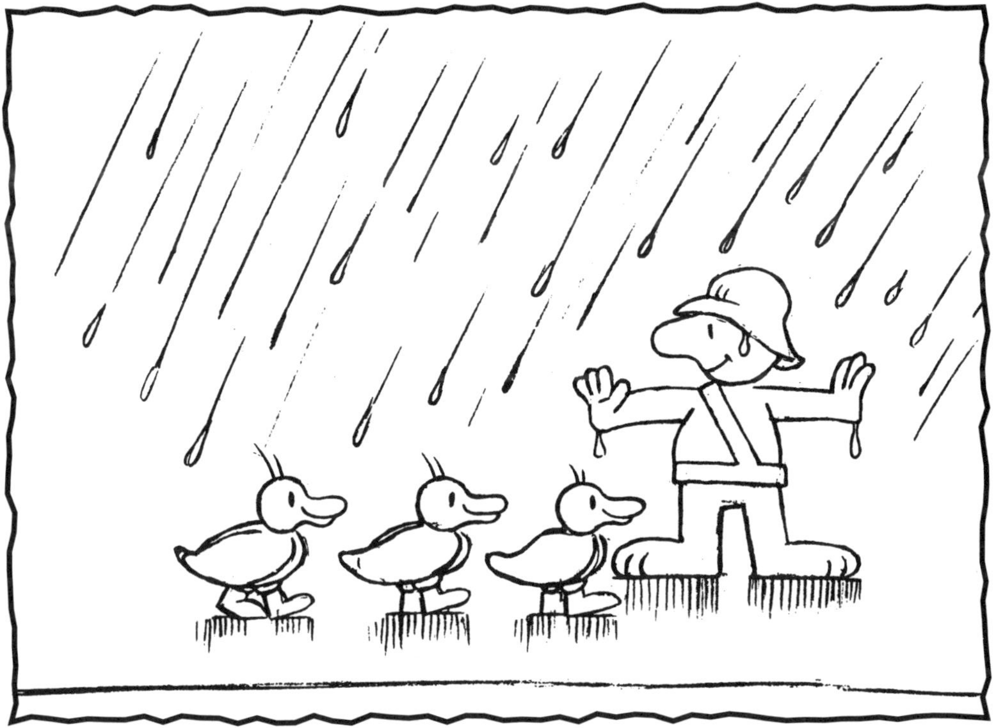

Remember the faith that moves
mountains always carries a pick.

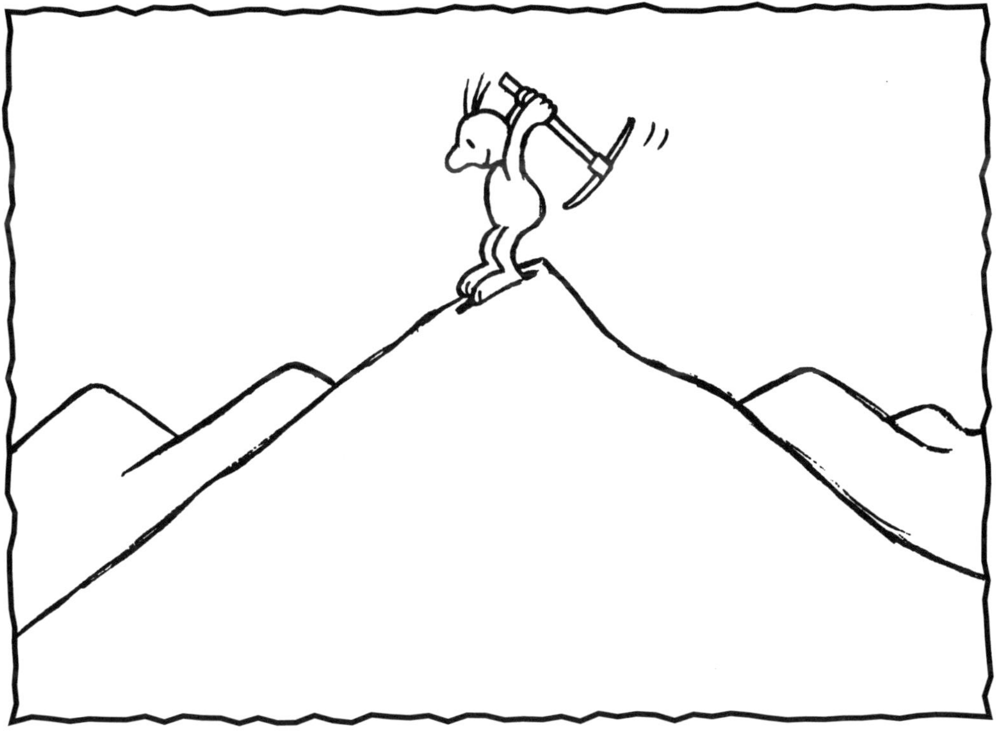

We cannot tell what may happen to us in the strange medley of life. But we can decide what happens in us, how we take it, what we do with it- and that is what really counts in the end.

Joseph Fort Newton

Lots of faults we think we see in others
are simply the ones we expect to find
there because we have them.

Frank A. Clark

Don't quit five minutes before
the miracle happens.

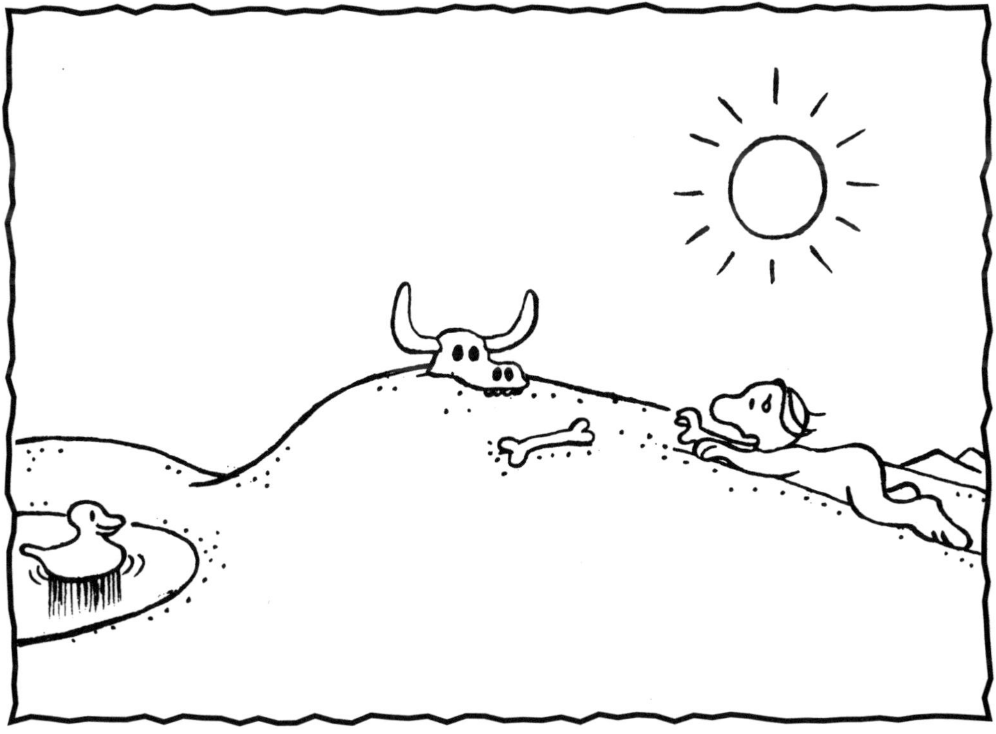

Always do right. This will gratify
some people and astonish the rest.

Mark Twain

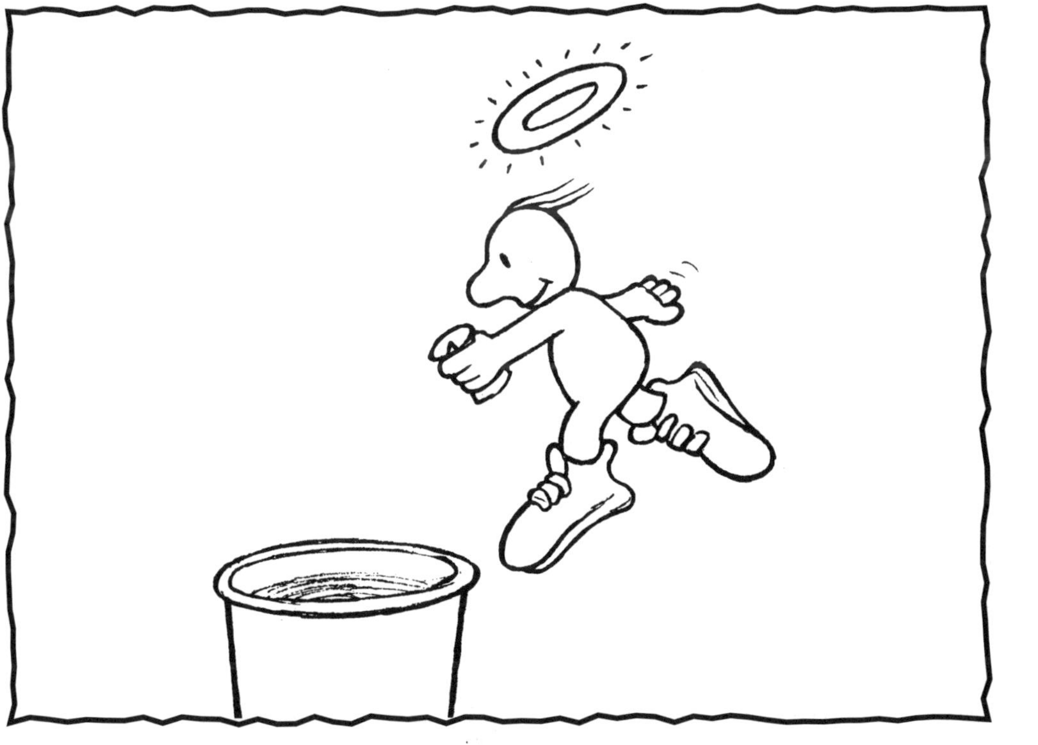

Some people are always grumbling
because roses have thorns. I am
thankful that thorns have roses.

Alphonse Karr

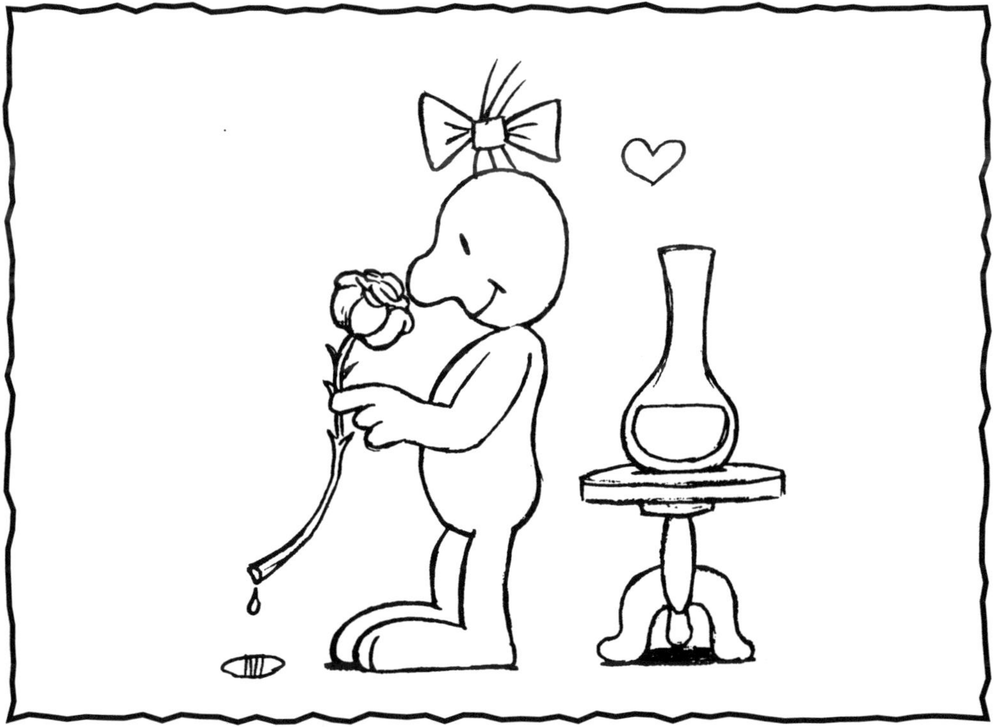

Believe that life is worth living, and
your belief will help create the fact.

William James

Don't let other people define your creative potential. No one, including you, knows what you're capable of doing or thinking up.

Dr. Michael Le Boeuf

In any project the important factor
is your belief. Without belief there
can be no successful adventure.

William James

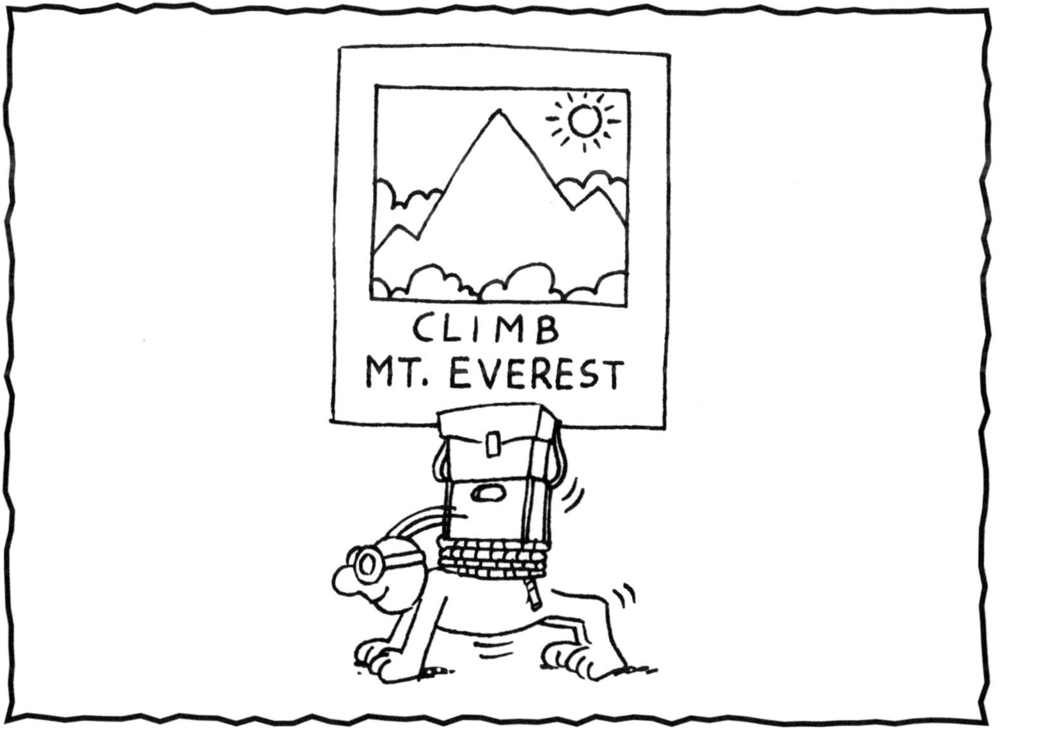
CLIMB
MT. EVEREST

Serenity is not freedom from the
storm, but peace amid the storm.

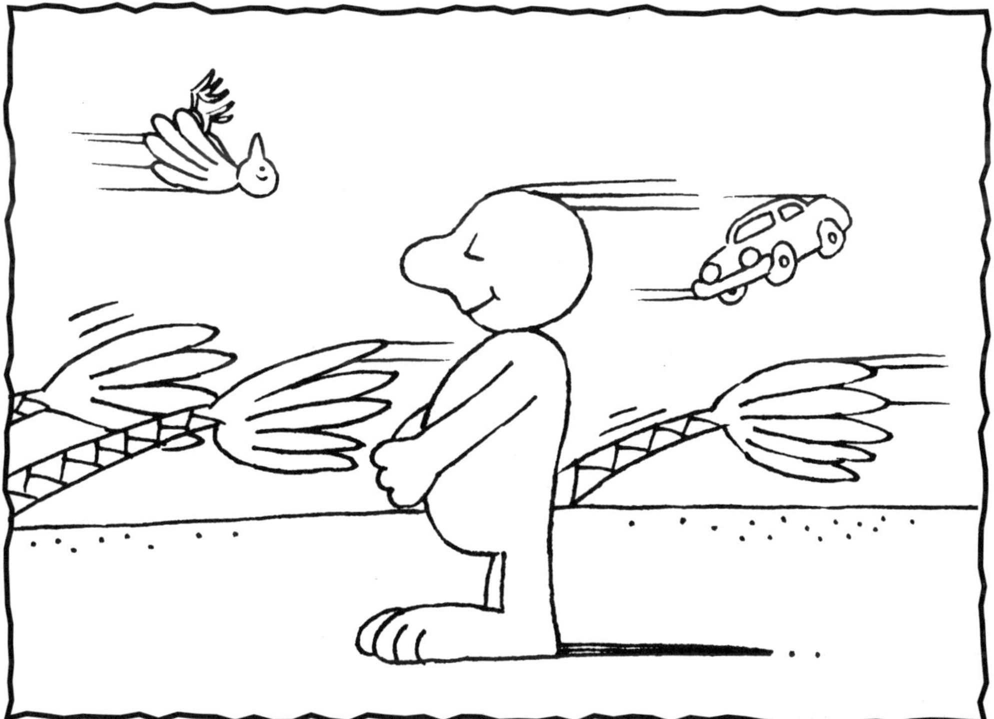

When I hear someone sigh that
"Life is hard," I am always tempted
to ask, "Compared to what?"

Sydney Harris

We either make ourselves miserable,
or we make ourselves strong. The
amount of work is the same.

Carlos Castenada

My future is so bright
I gotta wear shades.

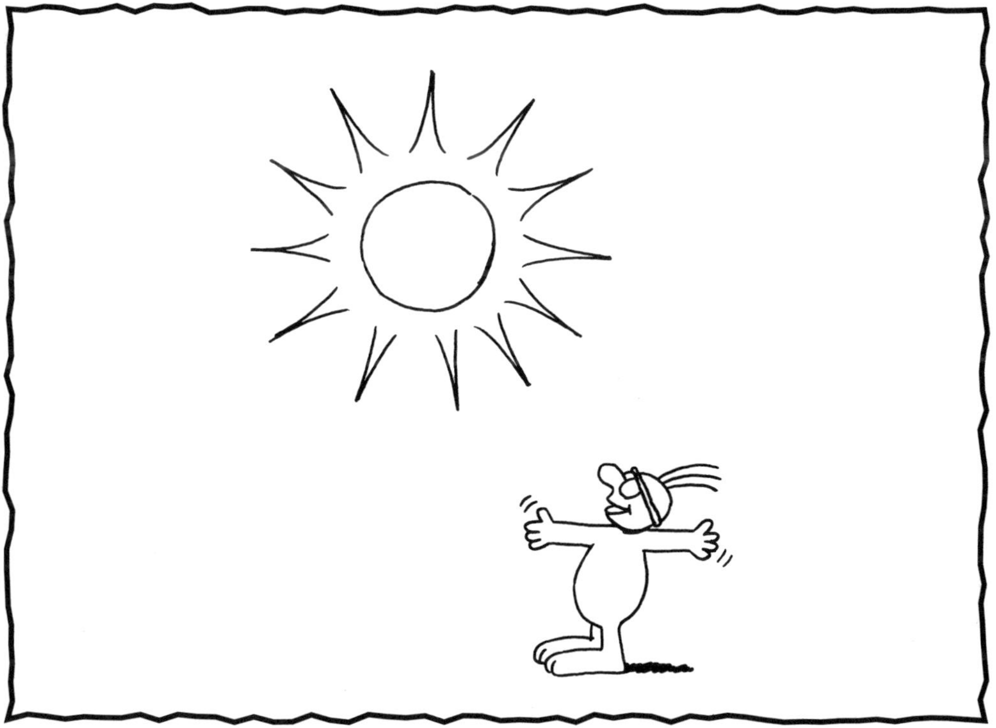

The most important thing parents
can do for their children is to love
and respect each other.

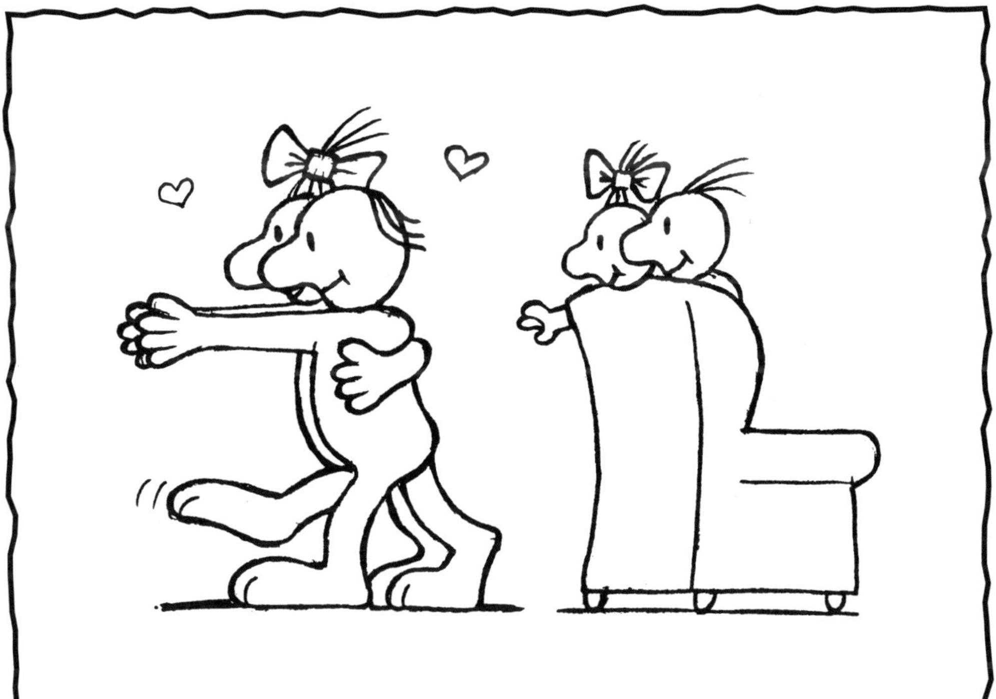

Shared joy is double joy;
shared sorrow is half sorrow

Swedish proverb

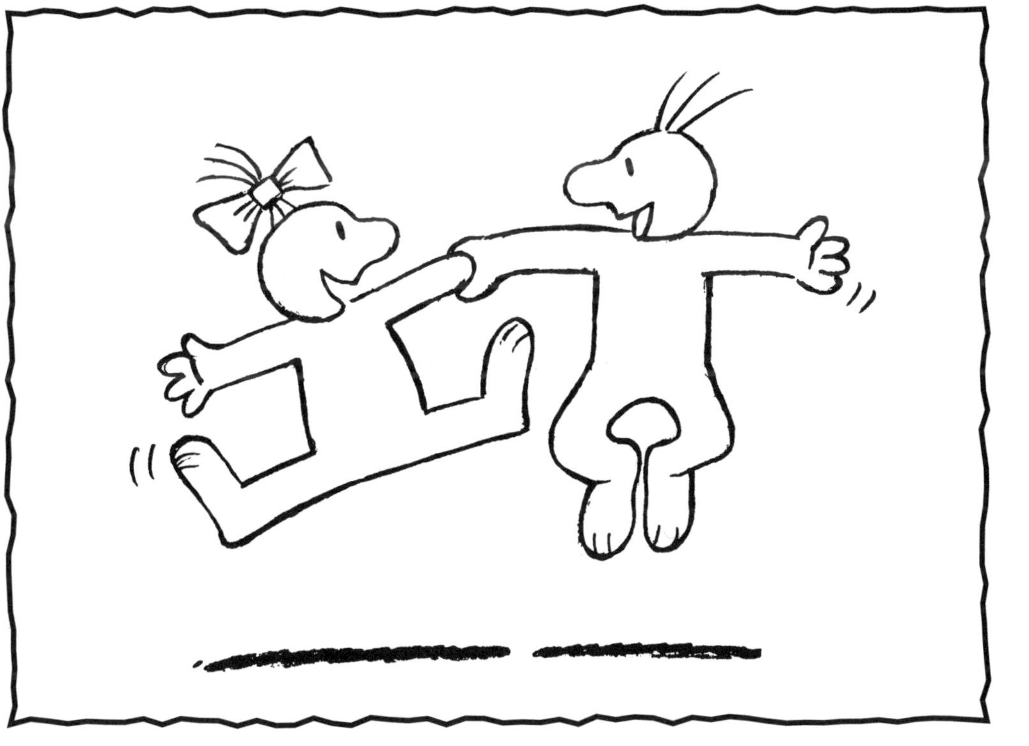

A rattlesnake, if cornered, will become so angry it will bite itself. That is exactly what the harboring of hate and resentment against others is- a biting of oneself. We think that we are harming others in holding these spites and hates but the deeper harm is to ourselves.

E. Stanley Jones

If you always do what you have always done, you will always get what you have always gotten.

Others can stop you temporarily.
Only you can do it permanently

Don Ward

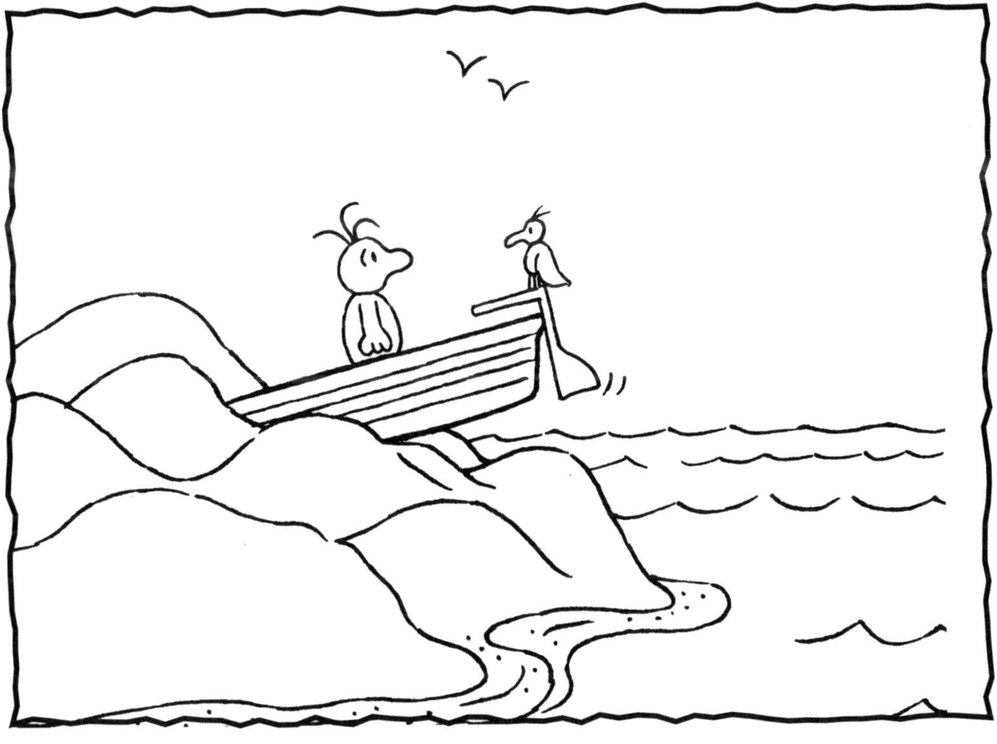

Believe in your magic.

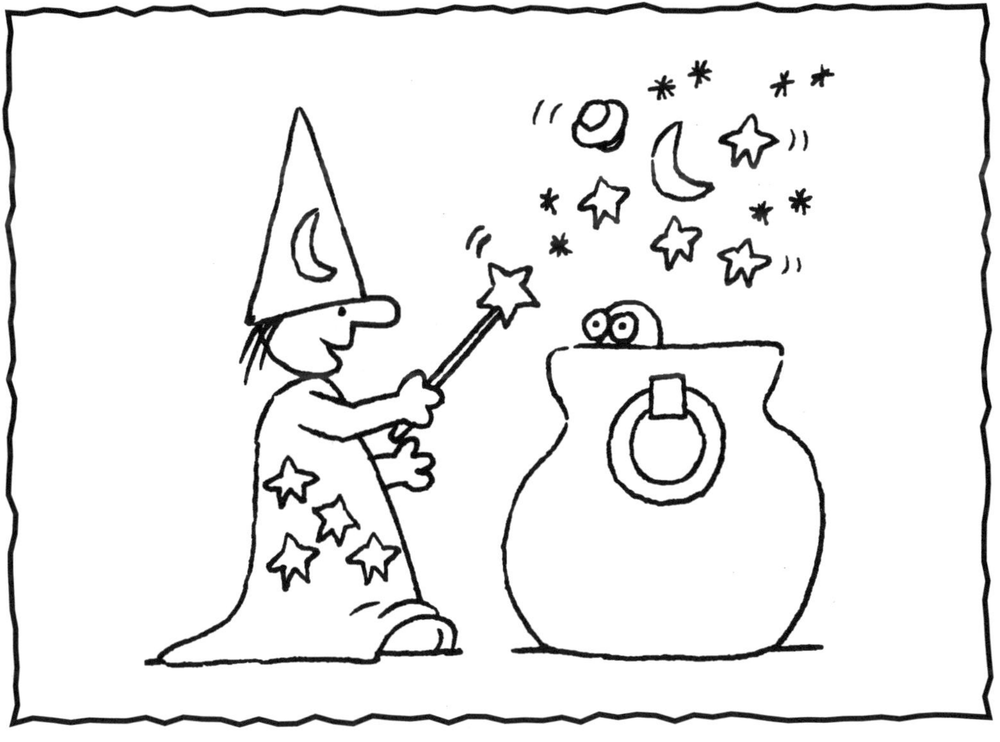

Once you get to be one hundred,
you have made it. You almost
never hear of anyone dying who
is over one hundred.

George Burns

112

How old would you be if you
didn't know how old you was?

Satchel Paige

I am a little pencil in the hand of
a writing God who is sending a
love letter to the world.

Mother Teresa

114

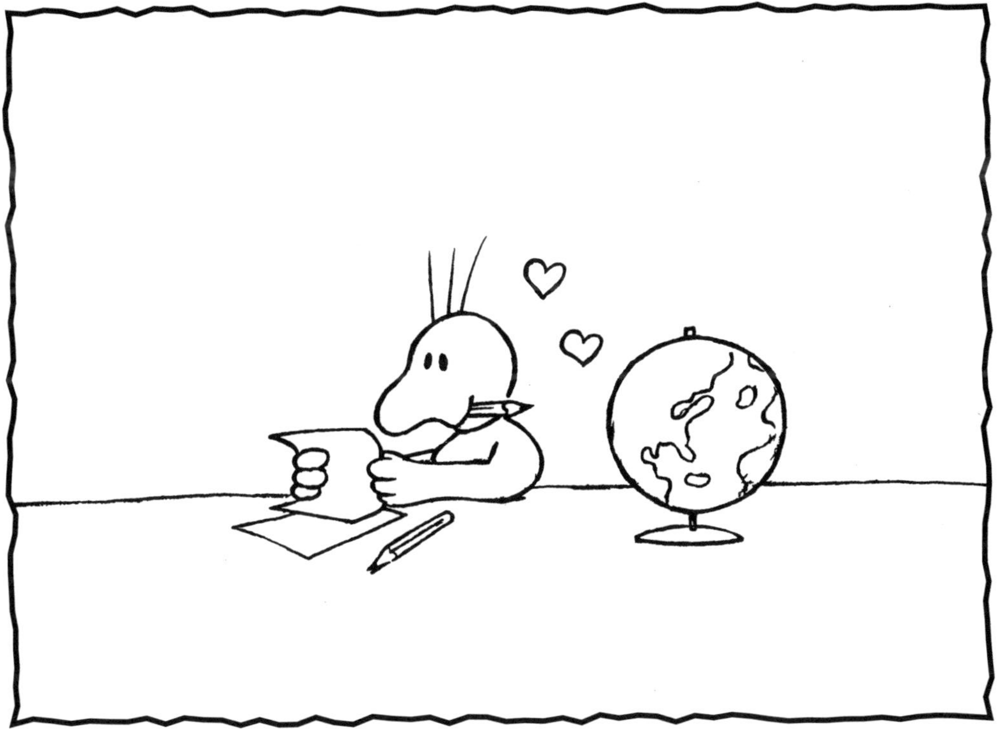

If you want to move a mountain,
you'd better bring a shovel.

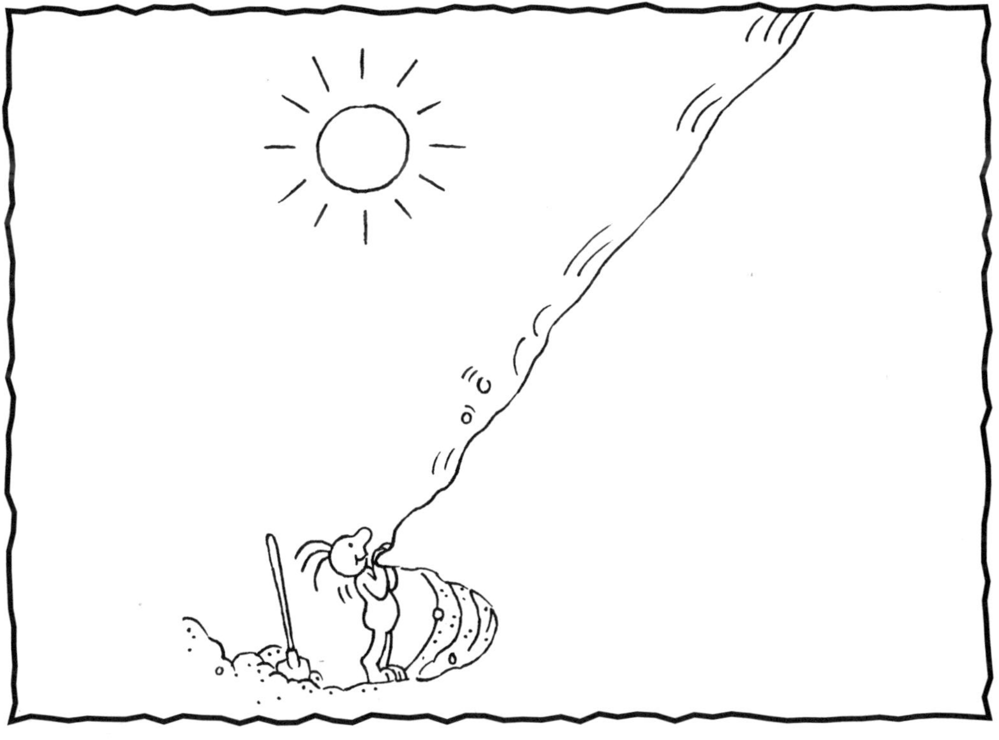

Enjoy what you do and you'll never
have to work another day.

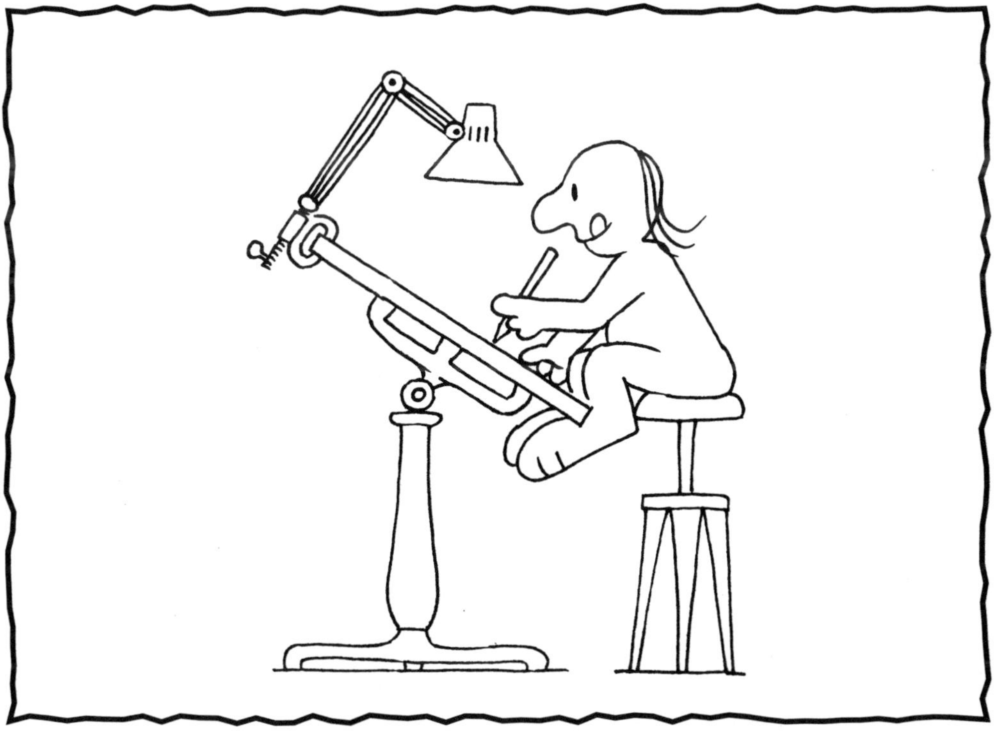

We have no right to ask when a sorrow
comes "Why did this happen to me?"
unless we ask the same question for
every joy that comes our way.

Phillip E. Bernstein

Be kind, for everyone you meet
is fighting a hard battle.

Plato

A man can do only what he can do. But
if he does that each day he can sleep at
night and do it again the next day.

Albert Schweitzer

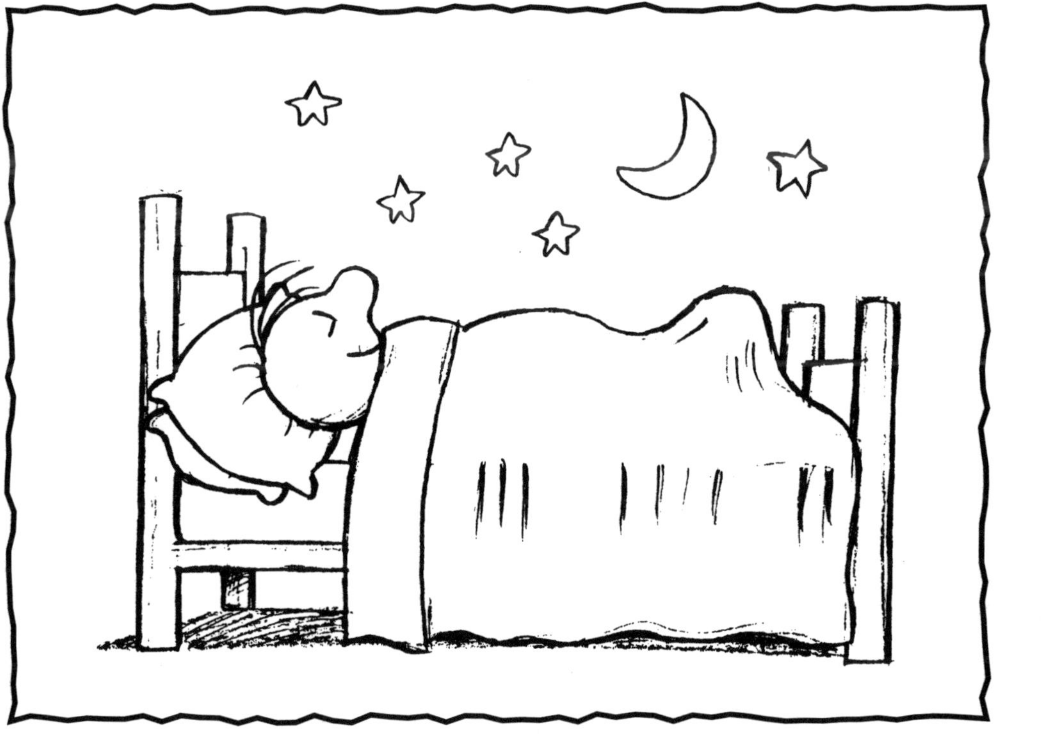

The great thing in this world is
not so much where we are, but in
what direction we are moving.

Oliver Wendell Holmes

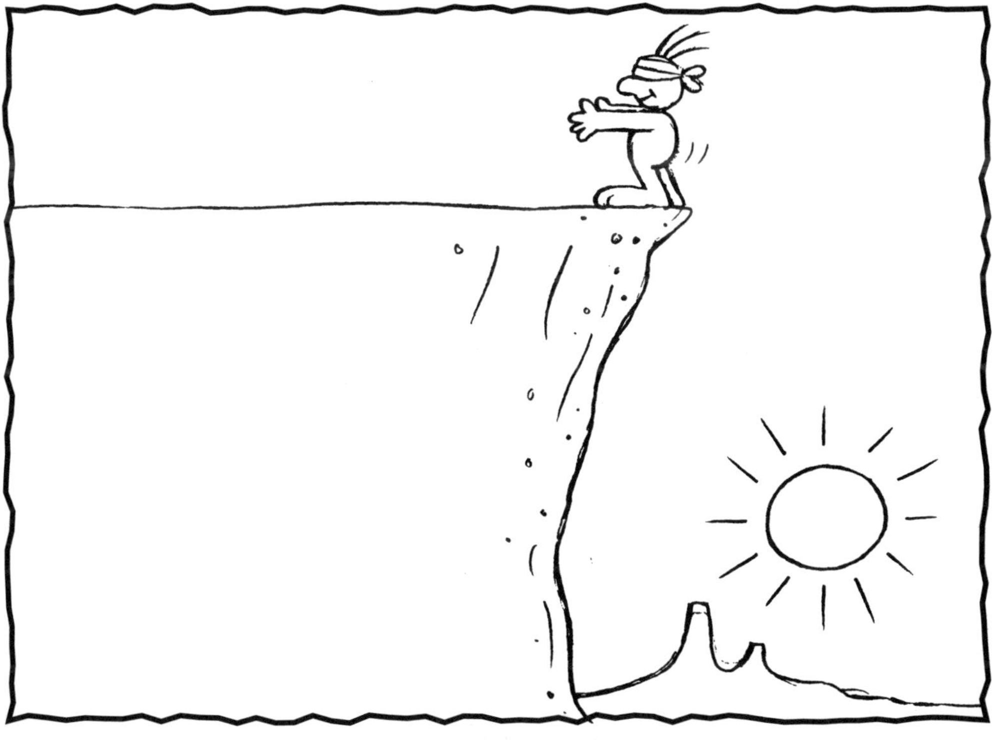

I don't know what your destiny will be, but one thing I know: the only happy ones among you who will be truly happy are those who will have sought and found a way to serve.

Albert Schweitzer

The difference between what we do, and
what we are capable of doing, would
solve most of the world's problems.

Gandhi

I am convinced that one of the
biggest factors in success is the
courage to undertake something.

James A. Worsham

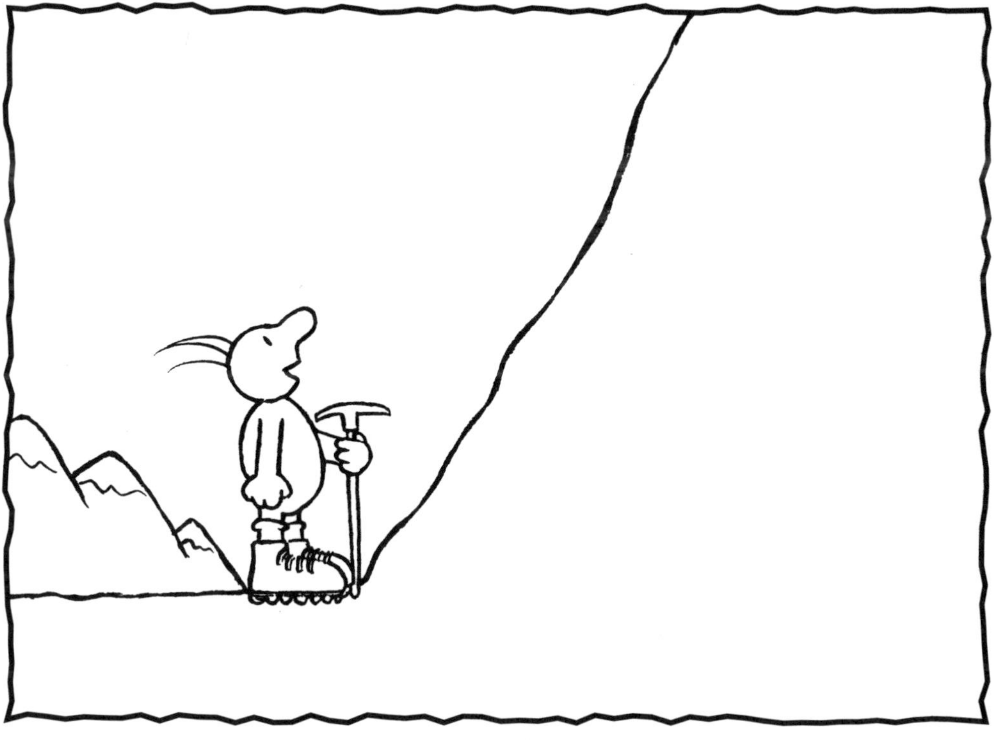

My mind is my garden,
my thoughts are my needs.
I will harvest either flowers or weeds.

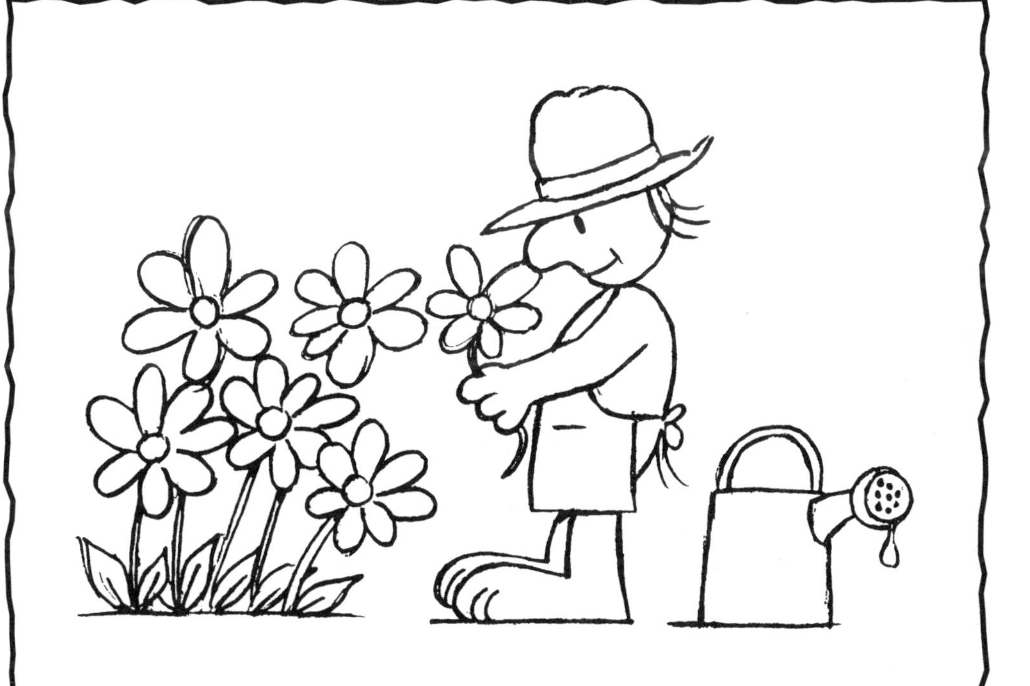

When looking for faults use a
mirror, not a telescope.

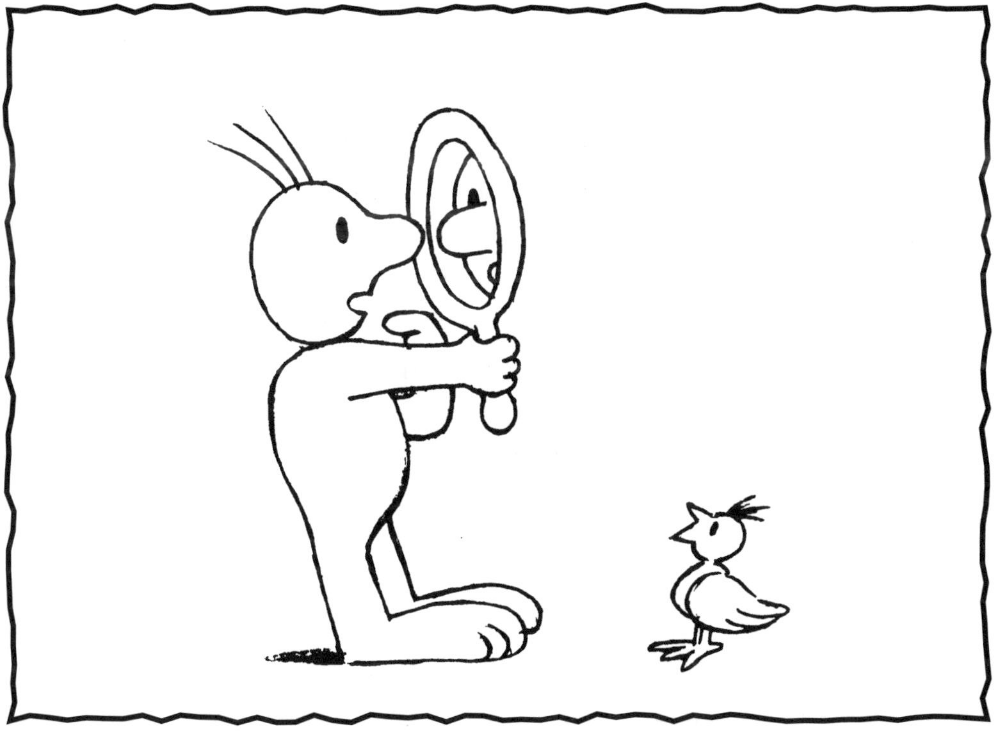

Listen to the mustn'ts, child,
listen to the don'ts,
listen to the shouldn'ts,
the impossibles, the won'ts,
listen to the never haves,
then listen close to me –
anything can happen child.
Anything can be.

Shel Silverstein

If it were easy it would
have been done before.

Jeanne Yaeger

Grant me the serenity
to accept the things
I cannot change,
The courage to change
the things I can
and the wisdom to
know the difference.

Reinhold Neibuhr

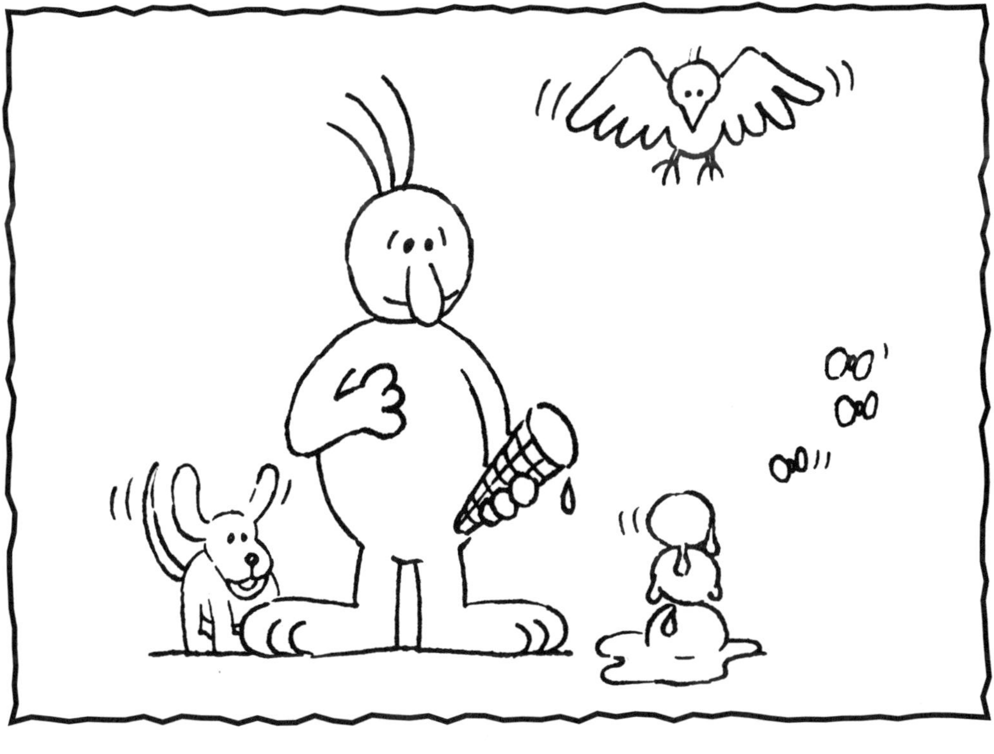

Remember this:
Very little is needed to make a happy life.

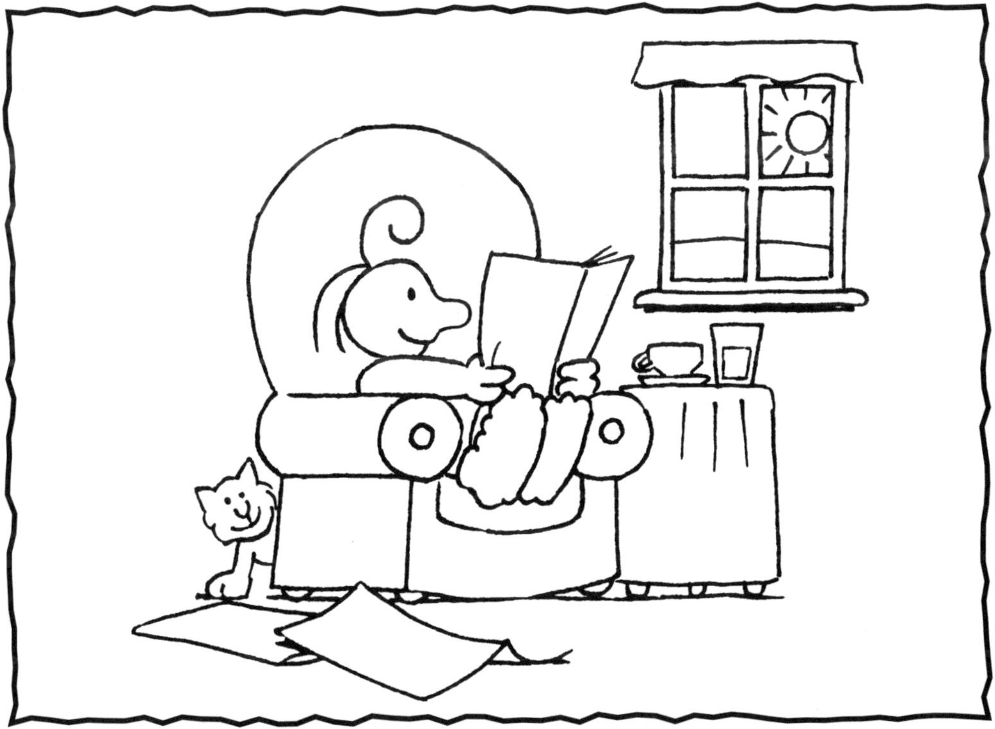

There are only two things to
remember in life:
1. Don't sweat the small stuff.
2. It's all small stuff.

It is not because things are difficult
that we do not dare; it it because we
do not dare that they are difficult.

Lucius Annaeus Seneca

141

Good family life is never an accident
but always an achievement by
those who share it.

James H. S. Bussard

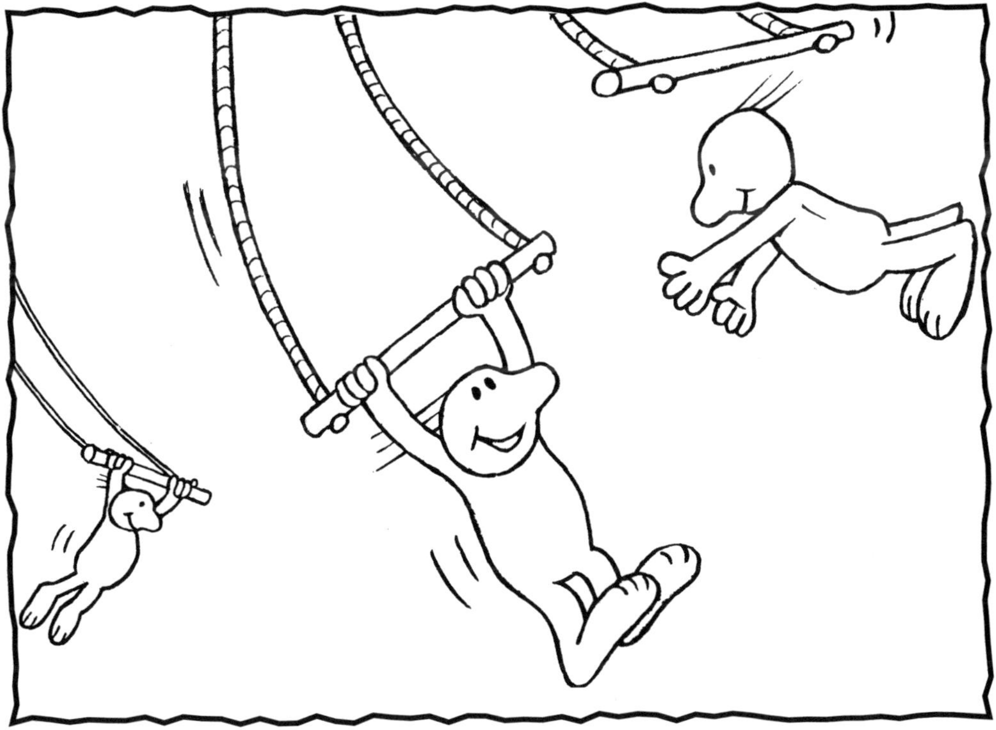

Worry is like a rocking chair. It may keep you busy, but it doesn't get you anywhere.

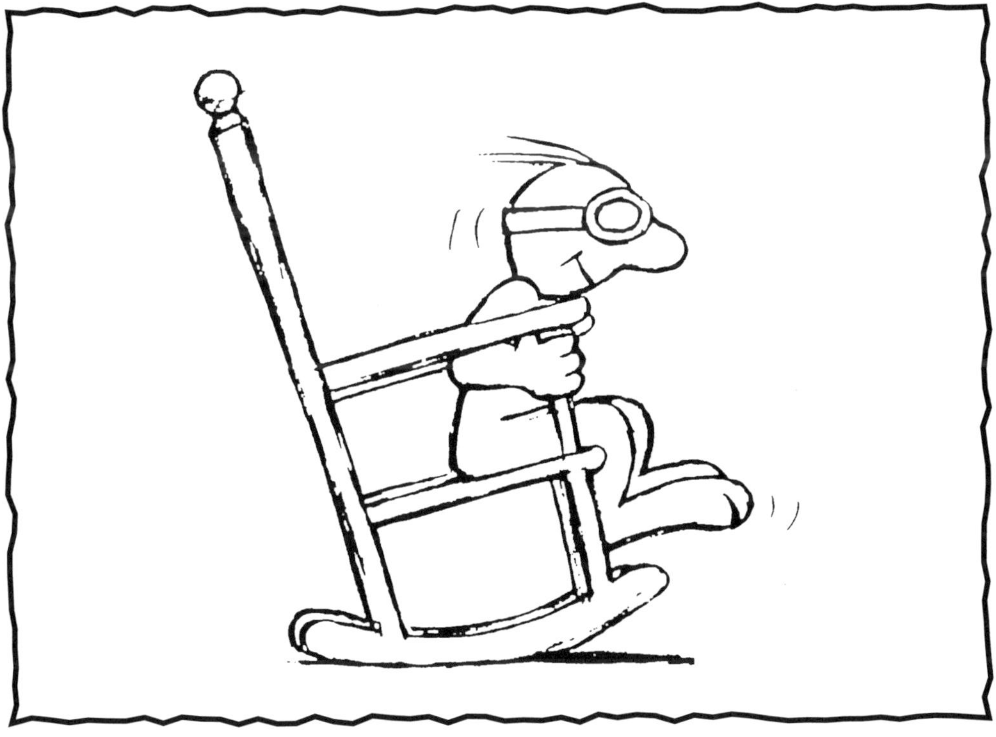

I expect to pass through life but once. If therefore, there can be any kindness I can show, or any good thing I can do to any fellow human being, let me do it now, and not defer or neglect it, as I shall not pass this way again.

William Penn

When we do the best that we can, we
never know what miracle is wrought in
our life, or in the life of another.

Helen Keller

147

When we fall in love with life, it
always seems to return the favor.

William Arthur Ward

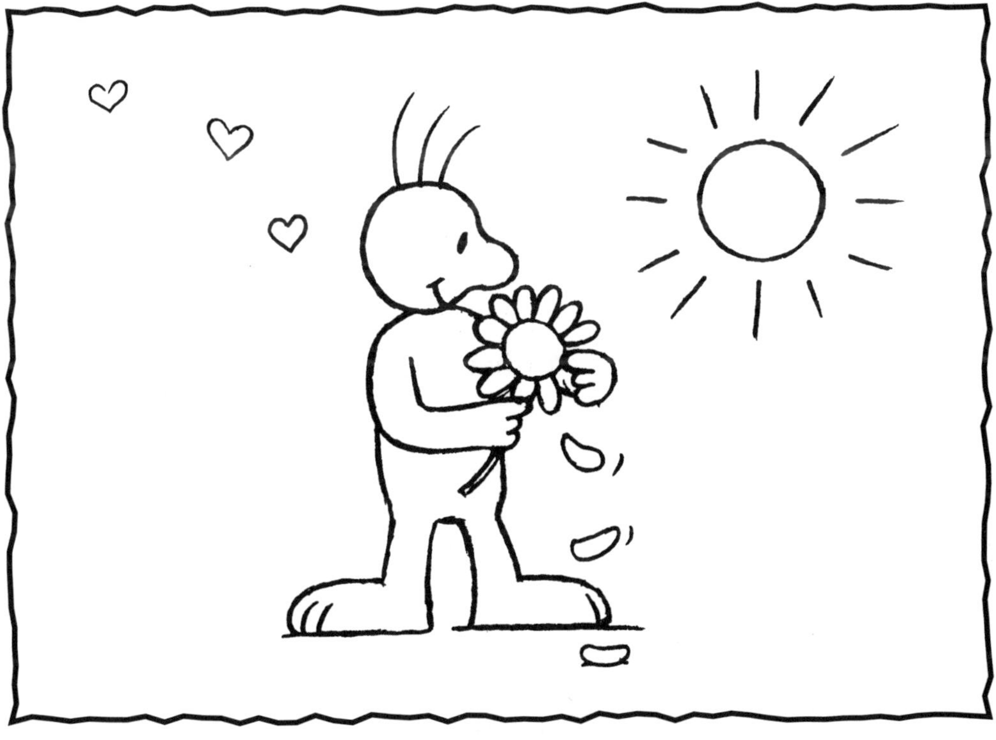

If you can imagine it,
you can achieve it.
If you can dream it,
you can become it.

William Arthur Ward

150

Any life is an unfinished story.

Ron Palmer

When one door closes another opens. Expect that new door to reveal even greater wonders and glories and surprises.

Eileen Caddy

152

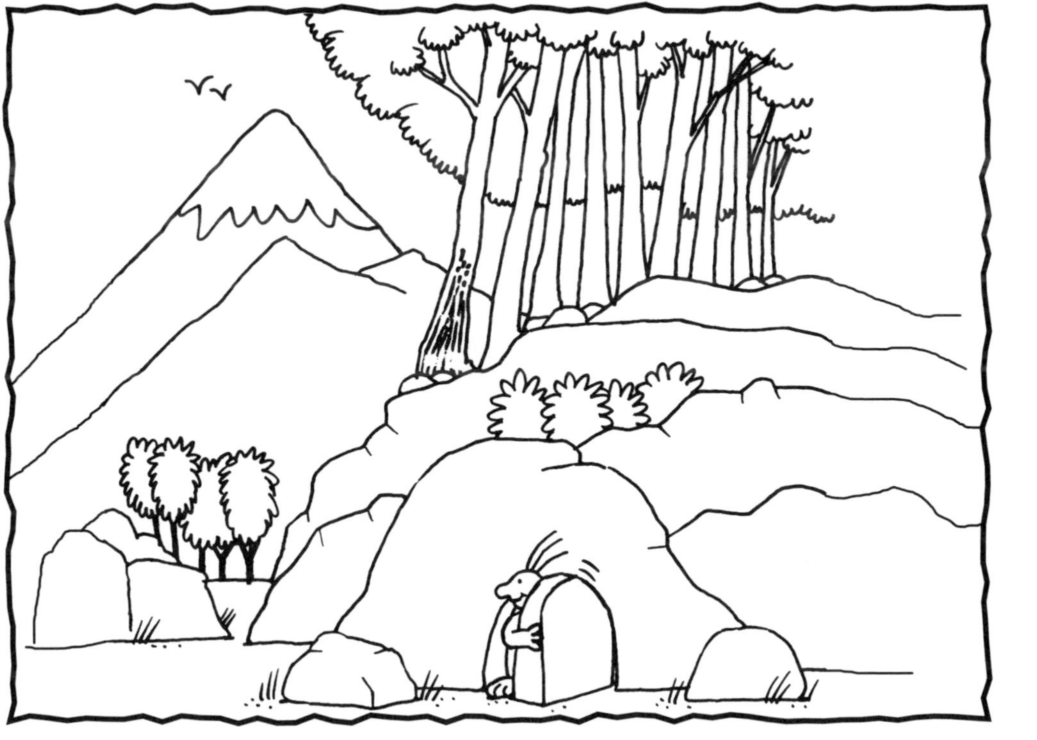

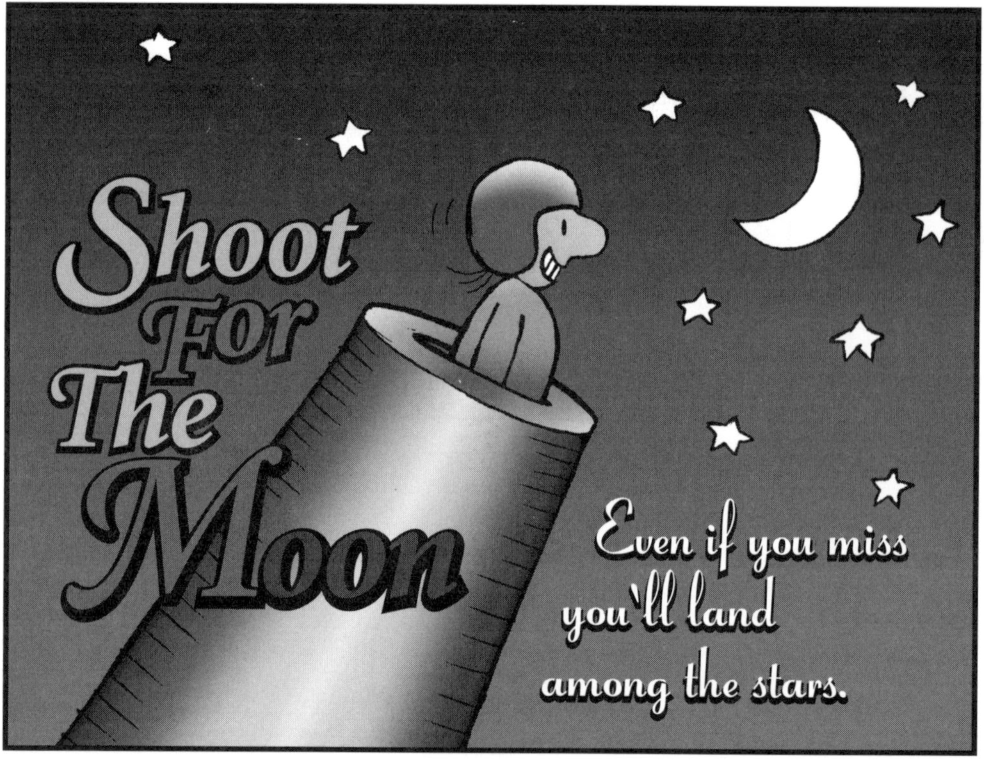
Shoot For The Moon
Even if you miss you'll land among the stars.

Children are Meant to be Seen & Heard

humor and wisdom
for honoring children

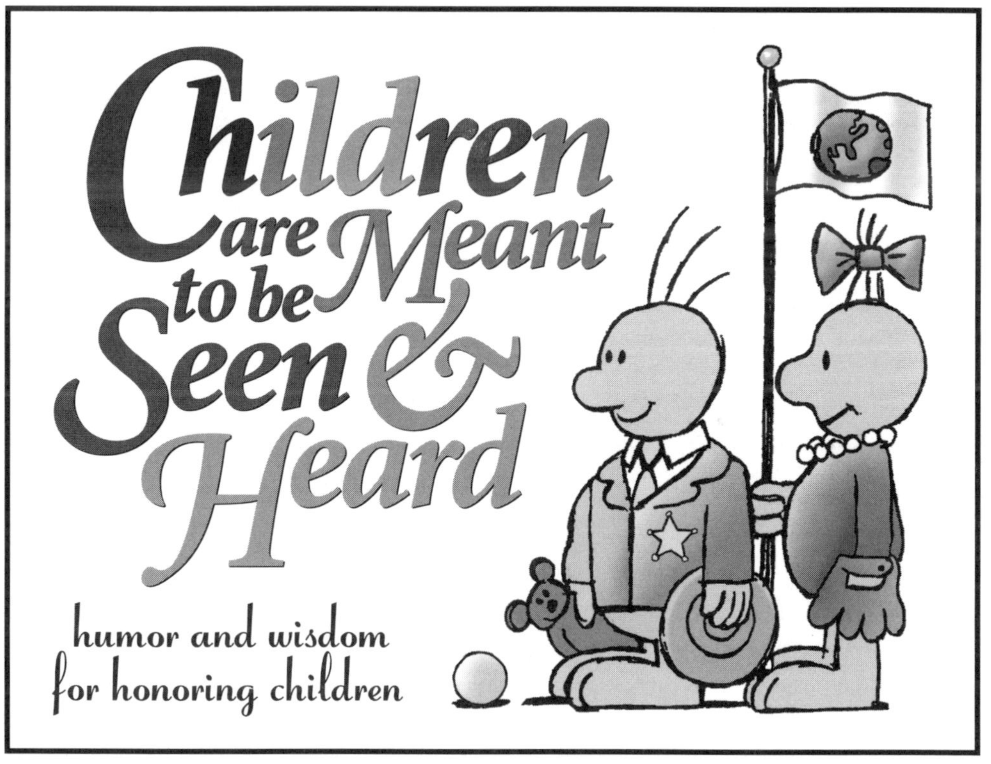

Relax, God is in Charge

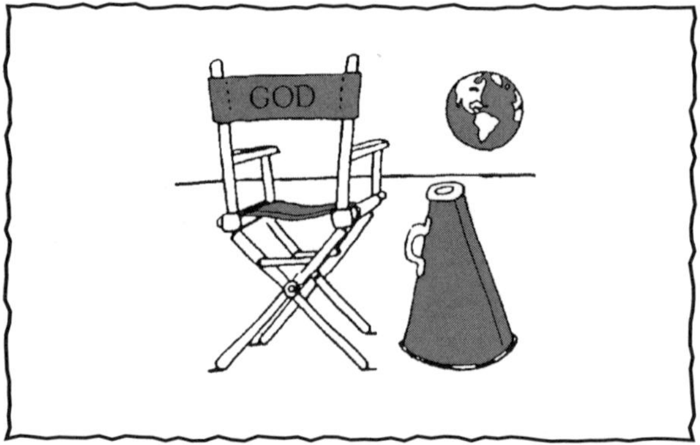
GOD

and 77 other inspirational illustrations and thoughts to enable you to go right, disable you from going wrong, stick to your ribs, warm the cockles of your heart and tickle your funny bone.

When Life Gives You Lemons...

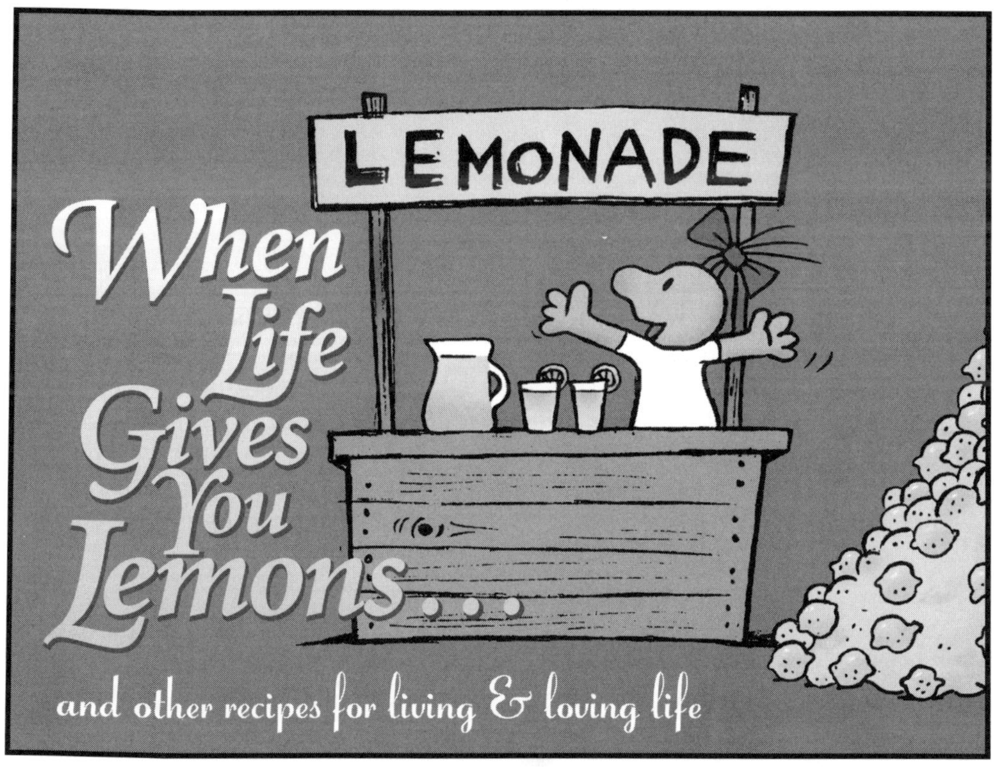
LEMONADE

and other recipes for living & loving life

P.O. Box 1204, Del Mar, California 92014
1-800-522-3383   Fax 619-452-2797

PuddleDancer titles available from your favorite bookstore:

Relax, God is in Charge	ISBN 0-9647349-0-7
Keep Coming Back	ISBN 0-9647349-1-5
Children are Meant to be Seen and Heard	ISBN 0-9647349-2-3
Shoot for the Moon	ISBN 0-9647349-3-1
When Life Gives You Lemons...	ISBN 0-9647349-4-X
It's a Jungle Out There!	ISBN 0-9647349-5-8

Acknowledgements

Every effort has been made to find the copyright owner of the material used. However, there are a few quotations that have been impossible to trace, and we would be glad to hear from the copyright owners of these quotations, so that acknowledgement can be recognized in any future edition.